TWO COUNSELLORS WANDERING AROUND A PRISON

Katie Carlyon

"Therapy is your answer to everything."

"I am a counsellor."

Acknowledgements

Thank you to my family and friends who read my blogs and a special thank you to my Ma, who reacted to every single one.

Thank you to Rita, my amazing mother-in-law. Your time, support and feedback will always be appreciated.

Thank you to my Jay – my number one fan who has always believed in me.

Thank you to Dave and Rebecca for giving me the best years of my career!

To all the men who gave me the opportunity to work with you; every one of you will stay with me forever – thank you.

Contents

Introduction

My induction week into the prison was a 'start as you mean to go on'. A prisoner had just come down from the roof he had been on for a day or two. A man had been stabbed multiple times – ambulances arriving and helicopters landing was my welcome to prison, and I welcome you to join two counsellors wandering around a prison.

Chapter 1
The Setup

I cannot remember my very first day wandering around a prison with my manager Dave, but I can remember the first few months and the many problems we had setting up a service. I remember having no office or storage space, so we carried a box full of our service materials everywhere we went. I remember the excitement some months later when we were given a locker in a shared area which perfectly fit A4 paper, pens, highlights, paper clips, pins and all our other stationery. I remember the list of 'things' that we needed, and I remember being left to set up this service.

Dave and I walked in one day in June; we had set a goal to run our first group by July. We began walking through the prison ground with our box full of stationery and group material and a writing board tucked under our arm. We ran our first group on the 31st of July!

The first group will always stay with me. It was a well-mixed group of different ages, cultures, offences and sentence types. As Dave facilitated the group, which was based around thoughts, I sat among the men in a semi-circle taking it all in. I watched as the men became more and more interested in what Dave was saying. I saw that they were starting to speak to each other, offering each other support and challenging each other's thoughts (in a positive way). I remember thinking, "I wish I could record this, how am I ever going to describe what I am witnessing and the power that therapy brings?"

The group went well with great feedback, but we knew this was not ideal as it was only offered to prisoners on that wing. Going forward, we knew it would not work; we needed to be able to offer men across the whole prison the opportunity to attend group. We were also aware we needed to be able to offer counselling across the prison. We needed a room.

We were seeing empty rooms everywhere we wandered, we never saw them in use, but we had not been allowed them either. The frustration was real and at times it felt like we would never have a place to offer counselling or group. I was very present on the wings; every day I would visit a different wing, which meant our caseload was building without having a space to work. Rooms were knocked back as well as ideas, due to risk and security and not being able to move prisoners from one place to another. We carried on wandering, looking for space and constantly thinking of new ideas.

All the while, we were thinking of referrals and assessments. We were receiving referrals but were unable to assess the men due to a lack of rooms and other issues. We had tried assessing the men on the wings, but it was difficult to find them! Work, education, visits and court all got in the way. We decided to send out self-assessments for the men to complete and send back to us via a different office as we did not have one. This worked and we soon had a steady flow of assessments coming back. In the meantime, we were still working out ways of running groups and eventually we found a way to book a room each week. The excitement was immense! This would be the same room we ran groups in up to the day I left the prison.

Getting a room to run group was swiftly followed by us finding an office. We asked the governor to sign off a room that was empty. I then spent the next month or two hiding from the person who had told us the office was not available due to her recruiting someone who would be occupying it. So, we could not use it.

I would leave Dave in the office and go 'gallivanting' around the prison. I sat in on groups from other agencies, on mental health reviews, and spent my time wandering the prison getting to know the environment I was in. I would go onto the wings and speak with the men with whom I would be working. Miraculously, in the November, I set up our first wing for counselling. I remember practically running to Dave from the wing, falling into the office, rambling on about the room and how I could use it once a week. By this time, Dave was used to my excitement whenever we got something new. Dave, however, stayed very grounded; we were very much like chalk and cheese in personality, but we worked perfectly together. This wing stayed my wing for the time I spent there.

I spent my time bouncing along to the wing in utter excitement and once a week bounced to our group room to facilitate the session. Group was slow and the number of attendees was low. One or two men would attend, if we were very lucky three or four. This did not faze me. I was just so excited to watch it build and felt we were heading in the right direction. Battle by battle we were building the service.

The next wing was set up relatively quickly after the first, we were now on two! While setting up on the wings it would take a few weeks for the officers to get to know you and for your routine to set in and for the prisoners to know you were a frequent visitor. Your time would be spent building rapport with both and building the trust with the prisoners as well as doing your assessments to build your caseload to commence counselling. If your face was not seen frequently, it would be a case of starting all over again. I will never forget the feelings of first setting up on a wing. It was a mixture of excitement and anxiety as some wings are more violent than others, and some are easier to break down barriers than others, but the feeling when you 'cracked it' is one of "Wow, we did this!"

While setting up, I built relationships with different agencies which were now referring in. The main problem was we were only able to offer the majority of men group work and nearly every man I saw said, "Miss, I need one-to-ones." This was frustrating. The men were asking for it, which was a big deal. The barriers were breaking down, yet it was still an uphill struggle to set up on the other wings.

The two wings were running smoothly, and more men were starting to enquire about group. We were growing, and we needed another counsellor!

In December, six months after entering the prison, we recruited a new counsellor. Rebecca came in with the same energy as I had and the fire to build on the service. For the next three months, we were a threesome and while Dave was in the office, Rebecca and I would go wandering around the prison, building the reputation of the service, and bringing in new referrals. We would visit the wings and spend our time speaking with the men, explaining who we were and what our service offered. This became our world for the years ahead and when not counselling, we would be wandering around bouncing from wing to wing, building relationships.

By March, Dave had left the service and Rebecca and I became two counsellors wandering around a prison.

Dave leaving hit me and Rebecca hard, we had all grown a bond and we came to love him. He gave us the wisdom from his many years of experience within a prison and that was difficult to lose. We were constantly laughing and joking, our office always being the loudest one. It was the first time in six months that I wondered what direction to go in. Within a few days, I had completely rearranged the service and Rebecca and I worked harder at getting the next two wings set up.

Rebecca was setting up her own wing while I was on another. We had now set up four wings and had each day in the week designated to a wing plus one day for group. We were established and we were building and counselling had taken off! The fifth wing swiftly followed and with each wing that was set up the excitement never dulled.

We had two more wings to go and then we could finally say we were on every wing and could start perfecting the service. We did set up in segregation but within a short space of time it became apparent that this was not suitable due to limited space and the sometimes-hectic environment that any segregation can be (this did change in the years to follow). That left one wing which proved to be the most difficult. It took over two years for this wing to be set up. The officers did not seem to want counselling on this wing and put up every barrier they could to prevent it. There were times I felt it would not happen and also times when I felt anger towards them. There were a lot of men on the wing asking for counselling which meant to us that the men were recognising the service and what we were able to offer. This wing was chaotic; the tension when you walked on instantly hit you, landings could not be mixed due to gang affiliation and debt and, to top it off, our faces were not known as well as they were on other wings. Whenever we would walk on there was an uneasiness with the men. "Who are you?" was constantly being asked of us. Despite the uneasiness, the number of men asking for our service was huge!

We did eventually set up on that wing mainly due to the

pandemic and it soon became my favourite wing to be on; the need that had grown immensely there helped the setup. The staff were never the most helpful, but we did not care. We had done it – we had set up counselling on every wing!

Even though we were overjoyed that we had rooms and we had finally set up on every wing, we remembered being taught how important environment is. In prison, we learnt it really is not. We learnt that by finding a confidential room and putting two chairs in it, an environment can be forgotten for the next fifty minutes.

When someone says 'counselling room' we often think of a typical room nicely furnished with a bit of colour, well-lit and inviting, a space that makes someone feel at ease. In prison, there is no such luxury. The counselling rooms were few and far between, especially in a hundred-and-ninety-year-old building. Finding one was like gold dust, but it didn't feel like hitting the jackpot! Our rooms ranged from cleaning cupboards, old cells, laundry rooms and offices. "An office?" I hear you say? They were often used for storage with toilet rolls piled high, keyboards and computers lying about, bags of prison clothing, broken kettles (a daily sight) chairs stacked on top of each other and, just to top it off, rat faeces! The rooms in the summer were far too hot (obviously no air conditioning) and there was no worry like I have in private practice of where to situate a fan. The men were expected to come into the room and bare the heat and they all did. The rooms were cold in the winter. I would walk in with a thick woolly cardigan with multiple layers underneath and still walk out with numb hands and feet. I would not be able to get the cold out of my bones until I got home and had a hot bath (something I was aware the men did not have the luxury of). When it came to something to sit on, we had fold-up chairs that were able to move around the prison with us. No comfort spared!

The chairs were also accompanied by my portable clock (due to my refusal to buy a watch when the Fitbit was classed as a prohibited item, the Fitbit being a watch that counted my steps. It was deemed prohibited due to it having Bluetooth and being able to connect to mobile phones.). My portable clock (also on the men's canteen sheet – a list of items that the men can purchase from outside the prison) became a part of me and was noticed by the men, mainly because Rebecca did not have one. One day she walked into one of her counselling sessions and sat down and was asked, "Where is your clock?" Her reply, "I wear a watch."

It was the men who tried to make our rooms as nice as possible. They would paint them and clean them, removing any signs of feathers and other remnants of the pigeons that occupied the room when windows were left open. We would purchase floor paint and they would paint it. They wanted the space to be exactly what we were taught, a clean well-lit room. Unfortunately, it was a case of fighting a losing battle in a place that is prison. Any spare space becomes a dumping ground due to the lack of it. We often went looking for a broom and a mop, and often carried a sponge and bucket to the room. This had become the norm. Having said that, we were buzzing, and we accepted the environment for what it was, wanting it to be better but aware that resources were just not there. We embraced the spaces that we had as our counselling rooms, where we listened to the man in front of us.

A lot of changes continued to happen with the running of the service throughout the years and we adapted to every change and every hurdle. For the first three years, every three months something seemed to change, whether it was how we ran or tailored groups, moved rooms or how we conducted assessments. We would receive one hundred referrals in a month including self-referrals. The service was known across the prison; our service had become what we had wanted it to become and it continued that way and we loved every bit of it.

What did not change was our office. We stayed in the same tiny office up until the day I left. It was filled with laughter, conversation and love. The small amount of time that we spent in the office built many memories and, in a setting that was so sad, it was our small space of joy.

We would have many visitors come in and join us in our little pocket. Rebecca and I had formed friendships with some of the staff in the prison and they would visit and have coffee and we would banter, have in-depth conversations and put the world to rights. We were aware many staff members saw us as 'snowflakes' and did not understand the work we did or loved but we did not care, we were there to counsel the men. There were also staff members who totally understood it and loved what we were doing. They would help us wherever they could by providing what we needed. Naturally, we would interact more with them than any others. It was hard building a rapport with the staff, but we managed it and we grew unique bonds. I feel this was because the staff members understood the men needed counselling and this meant a lot to us, knowing they understood that.

We would put the kettle on to fill our matching cups. I would put my feet up on the desk while swinging on my chair and let the conversation flow.

Our office was not on a wing, so it was also our sanctuary. It contained the work that we did in the prison, and by the end of my time working there, our walls were covered with letters and thank-you cards, and colouring that the men and Rebecca and I had completed in the lockdown.

Rebecca had also turned her hand to origami which I found too difficult and quite often mine did not look like what it was meant to be; these also decorated our space.

Our office also held personal conversations of our own experiences in life and what was going on for us outside of the prison walls and the issues we faced within them. It also held the complex issues of many of the men and the trauma. It was our space to process some of the things we had seen and heard; it was our safe place when, at times, the rest of the prison was not. We organised the service from that small area in the prison. Many changes happened there as did overcoming all obstacles that were thrown at us. Walking into that office every morning we were always excited for the day ahead and I can honestly say I do not think I will feel that immense joy again.

A year after first stepping through the prison gate, the service was where we wanted it to be. The service had been set up throughout the entire prison. Going forward, we would learn things, see things and hear things that we never would have thought of way back when, and on top of all that we had the woes of recruitment to come!

Chapter 2
The Betrayal

Janet joined the service and brought with her a whirlwind of chaos that we both were not expecting. Over the next six months, the service continued to move in the right direction and the group was flying. We were inviting twenty men to group and started doing an extra group day each week. Numbers continued to rise as did the referrals into the service. Our team felt right and the service seemed to thrive. The third counsellor was needed and welcomed, what was not welcomed was the devastation, sadness, anger and horror. Janet left six months later.

Janet had an inappropriate relationship with a prisoner. I remember when I was told. Shock is not a word that fully describes what I felt inside, I was devastated. My stomach felt sick, my heart was beating so fast. I was flitting between shock, sadness and anger, to the point that all I could do was cry. The overwhelming feelings hit me, and they hit me so hard that I did not know what to do with them. I became numb. I felt I had done something wrong myself and I did not know the impact it would have on a service that had taken over two years to build and establish.

Rebecca was on leave at the time, and I remember walking out of the prison in such a daze but also knowing I had to tell her. I knew Rebecca would be hit hard by the news. I mentally composed myself, so Rebecca would be able to say how she was feeling. I dialled her number. I cannot remember the exact words I said to her, but I remember the silence and I could sense her devastation. Devastation was the feeling that would last with us for some time.

We had been told that Janet's actions had no reflection on us or our service but we could not help feeling that it may have. We questioned whether the men knew and the impact it had on them and their therapy. The following months were difficult; we had loads of questions that we knew would never be answered. We went through shock, anger and sadness repeatedly. Every day we would think about Janet and what she had done and every day there would be more unanswered questions. We had an idea of the men who would know, and they had also been in counselling at the time. The men we work with have endured a lot of traumas and lived horrendous lives. This brewed our anger. I was trying to work through my own feelings around the client Janet had been dismissed for. He was a man who had endured a lot of traumas, and I could not help but wonder how it affected him. Counsellors are in a trusted position; men tell us things that sometimes they have never told anyone. I wondered if this had damaged him further. I worked through the guilt I felt around his counselling and how I should have worked with him, knowing how complex he was. This is something I have accepted but it is also something that I will never forget.

In the meantime, Rebecca was working through her feelings. She was working with men who knew about Janet and was close to the man also. I saw Rebecca's devastation. She had worked so hard to build the reputation she had gained, and she was working through a lot of guilt. Rebecca felt they were looking at her like they would look at Janet. She felt they thought she was the same which was difficult for me as I know she is the complete opposite, but I also understood why she felt like that.

Going on the wings for the first time after the relationship between Janet and the prisoner was discovered, our anxiety was high. We knew questions would be asked but we also knew, until formal dismissal was completed, that we were unable to answer those questions. We had decided that when we were asked, we would say, "We will answer your questions but right now we are unable to do so." The men accepted this and all we could do was wait. Six months later the time had come.

I had worked with a man named Kyle with whom I had built up a good relationship. He was someone who felt he had lost who he was after doing thirteen years in the system. After he completed his sessions with me, I continued to check in with him.

Months passed and he was referred in for therapy. I decided not to work with him due to the change in the dynamics between us. I had gone from his counsellor to an advisory role and felt that it would not be effective for him. Janet started working with him. Kyle was someone I needed to speak to. I was aware that counselling had been a big step for him to take and I was unsure what affect it would have on him.

Rebecca and I went to see him. Straightaway he said, "I have heard so many stories over the years and seen so much corruption, it is what it is." I asked him to think about it on a personal level and said we would go back and see him. We did go back and he said he had never thought about the impact that corruption had on him personally and that he had seen so much of an 'it is what it is' scenario that it became normal. He also added that he had told Janet something he had not told anyone, not even me in our sessions together. He asked, "Was she genuine or just offering me lip service?" A question we will never be able to answer. I walked away from Kyle feeling a sense of sadness.

Our main fear was that Janet's actions would cause the men to mistrust counselling. We had worked so hard to build the service and our reputation and worked even harder to break down the barriers that men face when talking about their mental health. There are a lot of stigmas around men accessing counselling and especially so in a prison where the overall outlook is not to look or seem weak. They have spent most of their lives building up their defences and we are saying to them it is OK, you can lower them, we are here to help. Knowing this and knowing some men knew about the situation with Janet brought us a lot of sadness. Out of respect for the men, we were ready to answer any questions as openly and honestly as we could, but it seemed out of respect for us that they did not ask any. We had separate conversations with those in counselling but on the wing the respect was seen and felt. We were able to move forward with counselling and continue to build our beloved service, knowing and thinking we would never get another Janet and the men knowing neither of us was a Janet.

It took six months of both personal group and individual supervision to feel we had begun to process the intense emotions we were going through and the situation overall. Both of us realised that we will never get over what Janet did and the impacts that her actions had, but we could move on.

Whenever we think of Janet, it brings a whirlwind of chaos and even writing this now my brain feels like it is filled with chaos. Looking back over the six months Janet was at our service, that is what she brought – drama and chaos. I can honestly say we will never forget that time but, for now, we were back as two counsellors wandering around a prison and had a bond and understanding between us that did not need to be spoken.

Janet was not the only problem that we had around our recruitment woes, and after her departure we were wary of getting another. We were happy as a twosome. But then it happened. Rebecca and I were told that someone had been recruited. We were anxious and that anxiety only got worse.

Chapter 3
Three Days in a Prison

Not long after Janet exited the prison, the organisation recruited a man who made us question what the organisation was trying to do. Questions came to mind. Were they trying to ruin the reputable service we had built?

Alfred was a character who is hard to describe. All I can say is he did not belong as a counsellor in a prison. Looking back now I can laugh as it is truly unbelievable, but for those three days he spent in the prison it was a nightmare. It did not help that Alfred was our first counsellor recruited since Janet. We were wary, on edge and were quite happy as a twosome, knowing we trusted one another.

When I say Alfred did not belong in a prison as a counsellor, I say this meaning both verbally and behaviour-wise. For three days we watched and listened and were blown away by how he got recruited in the first place, but we went with it and began introducing Alfred to prison life. Over the three days, Alfred had danced in front of the number one Governor, was rude to the manager of the clinical service, continuously interrupted the head of healthcare and did not take on anyone's advice or opinions.

We had to continually explain why prisoners were not allowed to have Skype and most probably to this day he still does not understand the reasons why. Whenever he asked us a question we would begin to answer and a couple of words in he would say, "Yes, yes, yes." Alfred had an air of superiority which he spread wherever we went. He refused to consider a woman's opinion or advice even though he had no experience of working in a prison before.

His superiority shone through and so did his previous work which raised even more worry in me. He told us how he used to take others' chairs due to them "not deserving a chair" as they were lower than him. He told us how he worked with young people and "knew what road he was taking" and described another young person while speaking about him going into crime, "Mummy, all I know is drug dealing."

My anxiety for his safety within a prison was rising. I was aware he was open to manipulation and following what we had already been through with Janet it was not sitting well with me at all.

While on the wings, Alfred's behaviour while speaking to the men was also concerning to me, with comments such as, "I have never seen a cell before." I could see how uncomfortable some of the men were. A cell is their personal space, and in prison that is their home. One of the prisoners looked at me and said, while laughing, "Shall we lock him in there so he can get a better look?"

I looked over to Alfred who was also walking in circles with them. I could not believe what I was seeing and once again my anxiety rose for his safety (as soon as we left the wing the alarm rang). On another wing Rebecca had asked Alfred not to do something, I can't remember what, and Alfred went and sat on the floor in the middle of the landing. I remember walking on and seeing him sitting there and just thinking to myself how is this going to work? I will never be able to leave him on a wing!

Rebecca was speaking to a man who wanted to refer in. The man asked Rebecca if she needed his number and smiled (underlying meaning 'phone number'). Rebecca answered, "No, it's OK, I can find your prison number on the system." Alfred overheard this and patted the man on the back and said, "Smoothly done." I was fuming! This could have potentially put Rebecca at risk and he showed no thought for her or her safety.

Around the men Alfred was intrusive, not just looking in their cells but in how he spoke with them. He would ask the men what they spoke about in counselling. He asked one man whom I was working with this question. Nigel looked straight at me, tense and clearly worried about what to say. I advised him that he did not have to say what he was speaking about, which inevitably he did not.

I saw a man on our caseload who was normally very upbeat, laughing and joking. I was aware Jason's trial was coming up and he had waited a long time. I also knew the crime was very serious and could potentially get him a life sentence. I noticed he was not himself, so I said to him I was on the wing for the morning if he wanted to talk. He thanked me and said that he was not himself today and prison life was taking its toll on him. Alfred came up behind me, put his head over my shoulder and said to him, "Cool shoes, man." Jason looked at his shoes, looked at me and then looked at Alfred, clearly not knowing what to say. Nor did I know what to say and to this day it still makes me cringe in embarrassment.

Some of the men on our caseload worked in the kitchen so we took Alfred with us. One of the men asked me what he was doing. I instantly knew who the question was about and, in that moment, I wanted the ground to swallow me up rather than turn around and see what Alfred was doing. My client obviously felt this and started to re-enact what he saw; he started dancing around with a huge smile on his face, laughing. As I finally found the courage to turn around, I could see that he was mirroring Alfred perfectly, I really was lost for words.

The language that Alfred used was far from politically correct for a professional working in a prison. Even after four times of Rebecca picking him up on it, he continued to use the word 'gypsy' to describe someone in the travelling community. This was one of the first times I saw Rebecca angry, and it showed, and it was totally understandable. It was something you would expect to hear from someone who is racist and prejudiced, not from someone who was about to counsel.

While walking past one of the wings he asked, "Where are the nonces kept?" I can honestly say that was the last straw for me. His inappropriate language had pushed me over the edge and I really felt incredulous! I could not believe we were recruiting this man who showed no knowledge of prison, no understanding of his environment and no idea of words that are used and not used. I felt sadness and let down, especially because of what we had gone through with Janet and were still going through. I felt if I had a job at that time to walk into I would have rather left than work alongside someone who, yet again, had the potential to damage a service we had worked so hard to build.

By this time the organisation was pushing for the service to become what they wanted – more group and in-cell work, generally looking at the men's thoughts and feelings and not counselling. I felt that Alfred being recruited was another way for them to say it will happen at some point whether you like it or not. Alfred, however, did not continue with the organisation due to not passing his probation, and was no longer a part of our service. Rebecca and I again became two counsellors wandering around a prison.

Following Alfred's departure, some of the men asked us where he was. Our reply was he no longer works for our organisation. One of the men laughed and said, "That's a shame, I would have corrupted him." I looked at the man and wanted to say, "Yes, that is the reason he no longer works for the organisation." Instead, I just smiled.

I was aware that Alfred would be a risk in many aspects of prison life. The men live on a knife edge and it would not take a lot for them to be pushed over it, not in terms of only harming themselves but also others. There are times in a prison when emotions run high, and it was questionable what Alfred would do or even say in certain situations, some of which had fatal consequences. I was just relieved we would never find out.

Chapter 4
The Questionable Ending

Deaths in prison you will never get used to, the feeling when you walk on a wing and instantly you are hit with pure emotions ranging from anger to sadness. That feeling of change and the look in the men's eyes, it is hard not to feel anything, and it is even harder to not take those feelings home. That thought was always there – is it right for a man to die in prison?

Most times, following a death in the prison, my walks with Rebecca to the gate home were in silence, but not consciously. I think we were both trying to process what we had just seen and felt on the wings.

For most of the men, counselling has an impact on their lives in some way, shape or form, but after a death, seeing the pain in a man's eyes, you know there is nothing you can say or do to help him. It is a process that they need to go through. Helpless is a feeling that comes to mind. Knowing that some of those men will never process what they have witnessed or lost is always looming. A goodbye is an ending, but the men never get to say goodbye. Tragic is the feeling. Some of these men grew up with each other and the pain they must have felt would be intense. As counsellors, we could feel their pain.

I once counselled Gary whose friend had died in prison. Gary had discovered him in his bed. The friend had died in the night from unknown causes. The pain and trauma I saw in his eyes was so intense. I saw him well up and then instantly knock it away and block the feelings. I know that while he was in prison he would never be able to process what he had seen. No man comes into prison expecting to find another man dead. He said, "I just cannot think about it." The irony is he had a fear of death and was in counselling exploring this. In his sessions I would use 'challenging' to look at situations and see how realistic they were. Working with a man who had witnessed something unbelievable, it was difficult to challenge him, he had witnessed something that another person in a different world could not imagine. His fear had become his reality. Death, and witnessing it, is a sad reality for some men in prison.

I remember Rebecca and I walking onto a wing, checking in with people not long after the deceased man was found by Gary. We saw a man run out of a cell, screaming, "Get help, get help!" All the men went running to find an officer. A man was fitting (thankfully he was fine) but I will never forget the look of fear on the men's faces and the feeling of fear permeating the whole wing. I went to see Tommy, the man who was screaming for help. He had just completed his counselling. I had never seen him cry. I was faced with his words, "I cannot cope with this anymore. I don't think I can deal with it anymore." He was pacing his cell, filled with despair. Tommy honestly thought the fitting man was going to die. Once again, those feelings and the impact of a man dying in prison were so intense; men do not go to prison expecting to witness such things.

Our first experience of death in prison (even though they all will never leave us) was harrowing. The men on the wing were absolutely devastated and we felt this to our core, the anger hit us like a ton of bricks. Yet, even in their grief, the men were treated as though they had no feelings. Whenever there is a death in prison, anger and blame are the main emotions for the men. We understood that the anger was a secondary emotion. All the men were truly feeling complete despair and sadness and the only way they were able to handle and control themselves was to react in anger, which most could cope with. Officers would say, "What about us?" or "Do they care really?" Such comments angered and frustrated me and Rebecca and showed us that some officers lacked compassion and empathy, not recognising that men in prison have feelings and emotions. The men hear and feel this attitude, so is it any surprise that, when there is a death in prison, the anger and blame are directed at the officers?

The men's grief is on hold and can be placed on hold for a long time until they are outside and, in an environment, where it is safe enough to open themselves up to the pain that is death. As a counsellor, I knew the potential harm this could cause, but as a counsellor I was also aware of the potential harm of opening up their grief in a prison environment.

One man I worked with, Craig, was new in the prison, and it was his first time. He was on remand for a driving offence. He did not understand the system or the politics of the well-oiled machine, nor did he understand how a death seemed to be forgotten so quickly. His friend had died, on a different wing, which affected him deeply. What also affected him was how quickly everyone moved on. It was hard to listen to him, knowing that many men who seemed to have forgotten the death had actually not. It was just another thing the men were unable to manage in a world where strength and the perception of toughness are everything.

I remember the mixture of empathy and sadness I felt when we were notified that family members were visiting the cell in which their loved one had died. I remember the men trying to make the cell as nice as they could. I remember thinking about my son, and I also remember the prison falling silent.

There are so many different factors regarding deaths in a prison, so many questions and different scenarios that can be put out there from the question, "Is it right for a man to die in prison?" All I can answer is, from my experience of the men who died while I was there, it was not right for those men to die in prison.

Some men managed their own bereavements while in prison. Many lost their mums, dads, children and grandparents. It was difficult to know what to say to them. We were aware that their grieving process, due to their incarceration, was not going to be the same as for someone in the community. Whenever a man has a loss in prison, chaplaincy would offer to light a candle with them. Many men found this a comfort; others, however, were not religious and did not take this up. On learning the date of the funeral, the men would request to attend. If a man had lost an immediate family member, he would automatically be granted permission (as long as he was low risk, including escape and conviction). I worked with many men who were brought up by their grandparents, often due to absent mothers and fathers who were in prison or dealing with addiction and abuse. In such cases, unfortunately, unless the grandparents were named as their legal carers, funeral attendance would not be granted. I saw devastation in the men when they were declined; the idea of not being able to say goodbye to the person they classed as their parent was heartbreaking.

Whenever we went to visit a man who had suffered a bereavement, I would often stand back and let Rebecca take the lead. She had a sense of calmness when it came to speaking to someone grieving. I would feel their sadness and the rawness in that moment. I felt that I wouldn't be much help, due to my own experiences of being bereaved.

The change in staff's behaviour towards a man who had a bereavement was noticeable. I suspect this was due to the uncertainty of how a man would cope – the possibility of him debating taking his own life in the early stages. Do not get me wrong, there were staff who were naturally caring, whom Rebecca and I respected because we saw the work that they did. But I suppose, for some members of staff, years of doing the job and seeing and hearing things chipped away at their empathy.

Rebecca and I would also be affected by deaths that happened when the men were released or transferred to another prison. One of those men was a man who attended group, he was a cheeky chap that pushed the boundaries as much as he possibly could. Rebecca and I would ensure he was aware that we knew what he was doing, and he would throw us a cheeky smile back. We later found out that he had died in another prison; the shock that we felt was no different to if he was still in our prison. The sadness of another life lost within the system waved over us.

I always walked to the gates knowing that anyone could end up in prison. In a split second, your life can change. I prayed that no one in my family ended up there but, if they did, I would pray that they do not die in there.

Some men had done so many years in the system that death was normal to them; it had lost its sadness, the shock factor, the questions, and the anger. These men had been prolific offenders on multiple different sentences, or your long-termers. The lifers.

Katie Carlyon

Chapter 5
A Part of the System

A life sentence…. It is hard to disagree if someone has taken a life. In prison we work with the men who have taken that life, we rarely think about the victim unless the victim is mentioned. I understand that justice for victims and their families is needed but putting this to the side what does twenty-plus years in prison achieve?

Over the years I have seen lifers who have worked hard to get their release and lifers who still pose a risk and should be in prison, even though the latter for us is rare. I have also worked with youths handed life sentences and I did wonder what this achieves. They lose twenty years of their lives in a system where if you were not a criminal going in you are one walking out. Premeditated murder is different to murder in self-defence, joint enterprise or even manslaughter, these are the cases I am referring to.

As counsellors we hear and see it from their perspective, we see the impact it has on them, we see the guilt and remorse, we hear the suicidal thoughts. Even standing in court, the stigma of 'being strong' is on their minds because of the place they know they are going to walk back into.

I worked with someone who told me during his trial that he was very close to tears and did not know how he held them in. I asked him what he felt it was, and he looked up at me and smiled and said, "My co-defendants, I did not want to seem weak." It seems it becomes something men learn to do in prison – shut down emotions quick!

There are two people whom I counselled who will never leave me. They evoked emotion in me. They were both young, both overlooked, both had the ability mentally to commit suicide and both were handed life sentences.

As I previously said, I saw a different side. The first man I worked with, his guilt and remorse were immense. Mark was on trial for murder and had pled guilty to murder in self-defence. Throughout our sessions, I had feelings of he needs to go home. I listened to how he felt, I felt his emotion and I honestly thought he was going home. Mark would continually tell me that he would not do twenty years in prison. This unnerved me because what is the alternative? Staff members did not really notice him, he was just another young man in for murder. When he was found guilty of murder, I was shocked. I was on annual leave when I heard, and I would not see him for two weeks – I was grateful for this as I honestly did not think that I would be able to hold my emotions when I saw him. I just kept thinking, what is he going to get from serving the next twenty years in prison? What is he going to do with his life? He is so young, is there not something else other than prison?

Mark was not your 'typical prisoner'. He had a mind way older than his years and aspirations for what he would do with his life – this was all over; his life had been put on hold for the next twenty years. My thoughts were, if I felt like this as a professional who can go home every day, how does he feel? Will he serve the twenty years that he said he will never do?

There was more to this case than murder and parts I cannot write, to keep it nonidentifiable. It made me think of the justice system. I really did not understand how they concluded that life imprisonment was an acceptable sentence to hand down. He was transferred to another prison, before I got to see him, following his sentencing. To this day, I do not know what became of him or how he is coping. What I do know is that he mistrusted the system and those in it and he would never tell the staff in the new prison his true feelings. He will be overlooked.

The second young man was also given a life sentence. Arron was a member of a gang who had killed a rival gang member. Even though his hands did not cause the death, he was sentenced on association. I worked with this young man and had a couple of sessions with him before he was moved off the wing and onto another that I was not able to access at that time.

This man stays with me because we had a two-hour counselling session rather than the fifty minutes that is usual in counselling. The reason – my watch was running slow without me realising. He explored a lot in his session, and it was emotional for him. I remember thinking of all the things that were explored; the time on my watch was not saying it was coming to an end. I did not find out the right time until our session had ended. I then went into the office, and they were beginning a mass move. I remember feeling confused, but I am also someone who is an avid believer that everything happens for a reason, and his extra hour was needed as it transpired it was our last.

Following Arron's session I knew his potential for suicide was high, but he was overlooked. He was expected to conform and get up in the morning and be eager and waiting to work. Some days he was motivated and some days he was not. He once said to me in one of the sessions, "Some days I get up and think I can do this, other days I wake up thinking I can't." I struggled to get through to the officers the potential risk that was posed by this young man. I was aware Arron had no family and contact from his 'friends' was dwindling, yet no one seemed to care, I put in iuku to the staff and outlined my concerns, yet this was to no avail. Within days he was transferred to another prison.

What stays with me is the men's vulnerability, but this was not seen, they were viewed in the system as murderers and that was it. The circumstances or events leading up to the murder seemed irrelevant to the system as did how the young men were feeling inside. I still think of them both every now and again and pray that they are making it through the system.

These experiences also made me think about the moments in time we have with the men, especially those who are given life sentences, and there have been a few. We would counsel them for a short period of time and then they are transferred to another prison. We will never know what has become of them in their years behind the door. We played such a small part in such a huge sentence. I often wondered, having seen the devastation, having heard the suicidal thoughts, having heard the guilt, having seen the shock and the horror, what are they like twenty years later?

We worked with lifers who came into the prison years into their sentence. Working with them it was sometimes hard to believe they had come in on a sentence for taking another's life. They seemed to have an awareness of themselves that was unique, an understanding of themselves, from years of therapy and group work to help them change and become fit for release into the big wide world they had come from many years previously. They gave us insight into how difficult a life sentence is and the hope that, yes, they once felt they could not and would not do their sentence; they contemplated their lives and taking them, but they worked through that and many years later were sitting waiting for that day they would finally be given parole.

The men also gave us an understanding of their perception of the system which mirrored all stories we had heard. This ranged from being set up to fail, having no support on the outside after their three-month hostel stay, easily being recalled back to prison, their experiences on courses, progressive moves and therapeutic communities. When someone serving a life sentence is recalled back to prison it is not your normal twenty-eight-day recall; this can be the start of a few years' journey to get released once again. The reasons for a recall vary from nonattendance to breaking conditions; it just seemed for a lot of the men we had worked with their recalls were quite flimsy and always had a story. We were not naïve to think that they may have given us half-truths but as counsellors we work with only what is presented. We heard stories of how the men were put into hostels for three months following their release surrounded by drug users, alcoholics, sex offenders and crime and again I wondered about the system. Why put a man in prison for twenty-plus years to release him back into an environment with such major risks? I also questioned whether this was the answer to what does twenty years in prison achieve? Were the men put back into these environments to test their abilities to manage and to not reoffend? Is this the idea of rehabilitation? I feel the system views this as yes, that is the expectation of the men to be released, reformed.

Men on life sentences work hard to get their release. Their behaviour is closely scrutinised as is their non-verbal and verbal communication. Behaviour in prison is a huge factor in release for a lifer but not so much for a prisoner on a determinate sentence. There are certain behaviours where all men across the prison could get extra days, and these include serious assaults and mobile phones. For the majority, six months will be the maximum sentence for a mobile phone but for a lifer that is parole knocked back and another year waiting. Smoking drugs will not get you extra days for someone on a determinate sentence but for a lifer, it could be another knock-back from the parole board and another year to wait. Any non-conforming behaviour will be logged on the prison system. These are known as negative IEPs (Incentive and Earned Privileges – note positive IEPs are also documented for good behaviour). Both positive and negative entries are drawn down from the system before parole so many men on life sentences try their hardest not to get any negative entries. While they are doing this they seem to lose parts of themselves, their thoughts, feelings and behaviours are what the system expects them to be.

Many lifers were given trusted jobs while awaiting their paroles, their years in prison a testament to their ability to 'keep their noses clean'. There was also another expectation of them, and this was to man the wing, keep things under control. Men often respected lifers, the reason being the amount of time they had served and how helpful they are towards men who are struggling, so many staff members were grateful to have one on their wings. Some lifers still had the 'old school' mentality when it came to respect and as the years passed this changed with the new prisoners.

Lifers, whether you agree with an eye for an eye or whether you believe in rehabilitation, will always form part of the system. They bring with them a debate and form a part of a system, and that system and what we were offering within in it brought a lot of thought and reflection, especially when we worked with them very early on in their sentences and at the latter end.

There are other prisoners who have to jump through

many hoops and are serving a sentence that I do not feel I can understand, they are the IPP prisoners!

Chapter 6
The Wonderment of an IPP Sentence

I counselled broken men, I counselled men who were institutionalised, I counselled men with no hope, and I counselled men who continually fought their way through a system... Who were these men? They were IPP prisoners.

An IPP (Imprisonment for Public Protection) prisoner is not provided with a release date from prison; they are given a tariff to serve before they are eligible for parole and they will often serve years over their tariff. For example, a man will be given an IPP sentence with, let us say, a tariff of five years six months. They would need to serve that time before being eligible for parole. There is no guarantee of release, and they can sit a parole hearing every year for however long it takes for a parole board to decide they are fit for the community. Many of the men I worked with did not know what an IPP sentence was when they were given it, they had no clue what their journey would be like, a continuous battle through a system, jumping through every hoop and navigating their way around obstacles that are put in front of them.

Their every move is under scrutiny, and as they get used to their sentence, they become aware of this. Mentally, the men I worked with were exhausted, they were tired of the fight, they were tired of the system, and they were tired of being in prison. At times, they were very low and at times they would find a new lease of energy to enable them to survive. In whichever state the man would present himself, I understood them both. I understood their new lease had to come otherwise their low mood would demotivate them, meaning their hope of freedom was completely lost.

There is not a lot you can say to a man on an IPP sentence. I was aware of the journey they were on and had been on; that little bit of hope constantly being dashed, took its toll. As a counsellor, I knew the only thing these men needed was to be listened to and be heard. I could empathise with their situation but could never understand what it is like to have no idea of my future.

I worked with a man who was on a five-year tariff and was entering his fourteenth year! His knockbacks from parole ranged from cannabis and phones to general non-conforming behaviour, but I also knew through working with him he feared release. Albi would sabotage his parole. He described to me that the last time he was outside he was a kid, he had never walked into a pub and bought himself a drink, he had never had a job interview or even a job. The outside scared him because he did not know it, the idea of going back to live with his family at an age when you are 'expected' to have a family of your own, a job and a house was evident in his mind. He described not knowing who he was. What he did know was prison had become his home; it was what he knew inside and out, and nothing scared him about prison. The scary thing to me was this was not seen or picked up; Albi had spent so many years in prison attending groups, completing therapies, parole hearings and meetings with different workers which would have been many hours, and no one had made this link.

Following our sessions and completing group work (which took a while to convince him to attend, due to him not enjoying previous groups), Albi once again worked his long way towards his parole. This time he had the knowledge of his behaviour, understood his fears, recognised his relationship with prison and knew it was a relationship that he had to end. He was transferred to a prison that he needed to be in for his best chance of release. Today, all I know is if he was granted release from the parole board, he would have spent at least sixteen years in prison on his five-year tariff.

Working with an IPP prisoner is a totally different experience from working with other prisoners. I listened to each individual fight through the system and, with that, I felt their despair, their grief for the loss of their life, their anger, and their utter confusion and disappointment. I would feel their mixture of emotions when they would describe to me how they jumped through every hoop possible just to sit a parole hearing. They would then attend, just to be told their offender manager or their probation officer in the community did not back their release so they are advised to come back in a year. I would watch them walk away, seeming much smaller than they were and knowing another piece of themselves had been lost in that parole hearing. The knowledge of staying in the prison another year slowly breaking them, all the while keeping my own feelings inside, I could feel their heartbreak.

Men described losing their voices and losing themselves. The expectation is to conform and behave, 'keep their heads down'. In turn, this caused them to not express an opinion in case it was misconstrued, to be careful who they spoke to in case it looked suspicious, to ensure they completed all the courses that were requested of them, to ensure they had water-tight plans in terms of jobs upon release, regardless of whether the jobs were what they wanted to do. One man came up to me one day and said, "I really want to do counselling Miss, but my parole is coming up and they will question why I need counselling." I asked him why the parole board would question it. He said that it would be viewed as a negative thing due to the many years of groups and therapy that he had already completed. This to me was incredulous! I am a counsellor who also accesses counselling! It was no wonder to me why most of the men did not know who they were and felt they did not have an identity. This had been stripped through years of being told how they should think, how they should feel, how they should behave and how they should speak. All elements of themselves suppressed because they were given an IPP sentence.

I worked with another man who had served many years on his IPP sentence. Wesley had been to many different prisons and completed everything that was expected of him. He was ready to go home, and his parole was coming up and it looked good for him, the possibility of release was high. Wesley attended his parole board and was deemed fit for release. He was elated, he beamed from ear to ear when telling me his fight had come to an end and he was finally going home. Then there was an issue. There were no beds in the hostels so they were unable to release him until one became available. With each passing day, I saw his elation slip away and as the weeks passed, he barely left his cell. I would check in with him weekly. I went from seeing him face to face to seeing him lay in his bed through the small window on the cell door. Each time I visited him I was aware there was nothing I could say to help him. Any other prisoner on another sentence would have been home by now and he was not. It took six months for him to be released.

I worked with three other men on IPP sentences. They had all been youths when they came into prison many years before. They say when you are in prison the time stops and your personality stays the same. I cannot say whether this is true or not but in these three men it seemed to be the case. They would all run around the wing laughing, bantering and playing jokes on others. When I spoke to them they were not emotionally aware and seemed much younger than their years. One of the men said to me that he felt the same as he did when he walked in twelve years earlier. I asked him if he was aware he was twelve years older. He replied, "No, not really, birthdays are nothing in here." The sadness I felt in that moment still hits my stomach even while writing this now. I did not know if, for these three men, it was a defence and their way of surviving the horrendous sentence that was handed down. What I did know was their journeys in the community were also going to be difficult to navigate and get used to because while they were sitting in prison, awaiting the parole board to grant release, the world outside was going round and ever-changing.

I totally understand why that sentence was eventually abolished but I will never understand why there are still so many men in prison under the conditions of an IPP sentence.

Men came into the prison both unsentenced and sentenced. For many of the unsentenced men, it can feel like their lives have been put on pause.

Katie Carlyon

Chapter 7
The Ups and Downs of Sentencing

We worked with many men on different sentences; the prison held those on remand as well as those who had been sentenced. Sentencing was a huge part of the men's world and raised many questions in terms of how long they would be in prison.

Murder is one of the few convictions that the man knows roughly what he will need to serve (if pled or found guilty); this is around twenty-plus years but for the other convictions it is a guessing game.

Men would go by the guidelines laid out by the solicitors or what their peers had been sentenced to previously. Some came back from court happy with their sentences, but many did not, especially when they compared the sentence to others who had gotten a lot less.

At the time I was working in the prison, drug dealing had become a huge issue in society and the sentences handed down were getting heftier. Some men said it depended on which judge you got, others said that didn't matter and it depended on the mood of the judge on the day.

I worked with men whose sentences had shocked me but had made them happy, which I did not understand. One of the men I was working with was concerned about his relationship. Kurt was looking at a long time in prison and was unsure whether his partner would wait for him. I went to visit him the day after he got sentenced. I had seen on the prison system that he had got fourteen years. I was taken aback by how happy he was. Kurt said he was really pleased with the outcome and was now looking to transfer out and get on with his time. It surprised me each time how the men were resilient in terms of accepting their time and getting on with it. I would walk around the prison feeling I could never live in a place like that and could not see myself accepting it as my world for a huge chunk of my life.

I worked with another man who had pled not guilty to his crime. Bailey said he was guilty of some of the charges but not all of them. He was paying a good solicitor and was willing to fight. This would be his second strike for the same offence so if he was found guilty, he was looking at a big sentence, over ten years. A week or so before his court hearing I went to see him, and Bailey told me he had pled guilty. I remember feeling confused, I asked him why if he were not guilty would he say he was? He said his solicitor had advised him that there was a possibility that he could be found guilty by the jury. If he pled guilty, he would get less time so that is what he decided to do. He got sentenced to seven years and was pleased with the outcome.

It made me once again question the system. The men were pleading guilty to offences they did not commit to reduce their sentence time in case they were found guilty. How is this justice? Unfortunately, as the years went by, I came to realise that this is the system, and many men would plead guilty and put forward their mitigating circumstances for a reduced sentence.

On the flip side, this also included the most heinous of crimes – sexual offences. This brewed anger across the prison. Many drug dealers were getting higher sentences than sex offenders and many sex offenders came back with what was seen as 'lenient' sentences due to their early guilty pleas.

I did understand the anger. I worked with the sex offenders, and I can honestly say their sentences were pitiful, especially if they were compared to those in general population. On many occasions, their sentences did not reflect the impact their actions had on their victims and will have for the rest of their lives. Sex offenders and their sentences will always be an issue across the prison as long as their sentences remain so lenient.

For the men on murder charges, Rebecca and I understood that they would come back into the prison at one of their lowest points. What do you say to a man who has been given twenty-something years in prison? Not a lot. We would advise that we were there if they needed us and would regularly visit them until they were transferred out. We watched men take it in their stride, with some kind of odd acceptance that this is where their future lies. We watched men self-destruct, taking whatever drugs they could get their hands on to take them out of the harsh reality that their actions had not only taken a life but cost them their own.

Comparing sentences for the men was not always the best option. They would go on what others came back from court with, often causing themselves disappointment when their time came. One of the men I worked with was in for a violent offence, it was Drew's first time in prison. He had already pled guilty and was awaiting sentencing. Drew told me he thought he was only looking at a couple of years, based on what he had heard others had previously got. I remember thinking that this man was potentially looking at a long time. His charge had been dropped from attempted murder but was still a big charge. I remember thinking, why has his solicitor not advised him of this? As it turned out he got nine years, and this hit him hard. The anxiety he was living with was high. He was unable to control his overthinking or his panic. Drew was in the place where many men found themselves after being sentenced and not understanding it. The feeling of being stuck.

Not understanding the sentence and being stuck on it was detrimental to many of the men. They were wrapped up in a sentence that was not going to change. They would get their hopes up while entering their appeals which nine times out of ten were knocked back. A man could appeal the first time and appeal the second but on the second the judge could rule that they start the sentence again. This put off many men from attempting a second appeal, leaving them to wonder whether they would have won that appeal or not.

Many men walked around feeling the injustice of the system and, for some, it took a long time to move forward from this. Rebecca and I would sit with some of them for weeks and they would repeat what they had said the week before, trying to fathom what had happened and why the system was the way it was.

We understood that it was a process the men needed to go through, not only for their mental health but to be able to survive the years ahead of them. The men needed to process that, for many years ahead, prison was where they were going to be and for some it was hard to believe.

I worked with a man who had got ten years for his offence. Simon was in shock and could not believe it. It took many weeks of counselling for him to process it, the number ten had become a huge part of his life and he noticed the number wherever it appeared. Simon had a tough couple of years awaiting sentencing, re-categorisation and transferring, not including what he endured personally and emotionally. When his time did come and he was transferring to another prison, Rebecca and I visited him in the holding cell. He looked like a different person. He was focused and set for his journey and that journey would lead him to home. There were times that I felt Simon may never accept his sentence and he would remain stuck, but I relied on his counselling journey to aid this and it did. It gave me and Rebecca hope for many men who would enter the prison and live a similar journey.

Seeing these men begin their journeys after sentencing made me reflect more on the idea of the system and what it is, or even what it is meant to be, and everywhere I looked all I could see was rehabilitation.

Katie Carlyon

Chapter 8
Rehabilitation?

Counselling the men, we got an insight into their world. I will always feel humbled by them letting me be a part of that. I have heard of horrendous abuse including physical, sexual and emotional. Extreme forms of neglect and fight baiting. I have also heard about corruption and abuse within our systems. They included young offenders' institutions, the care system, the prison system, and the overall justice system. It always brought to my mind the question: Is there passion for rehabilitation?

I will never forget when a man said to me, "The system has broken me. I am done now. I have learnt my lesson. I want to go home." Some may call that rehabilitation, but I know he had seen someone die, heard of two others kill themselves, was accused of a serious assault he did not commit and was a victim of a serious assault himself, all of which happened within two years.... would you still say rehabilitated?

I counselled David, who had been found not guilty of a crime but still had to wait to sit a parole board to fight for his release because of his IPP sentence which had previously been abolished. David's words to me were, "I am going to die in here." Would you say rehabilitated? I have seen the rise of joint enterprise within the system and the impacts that it has. Joint enterprise is when an offence is committed and more than one person is convicted for that crime. This could be because they were seen to encourage the offence and/or had some kind of involvement in it.

I counselled a young man who had been convicted of murder through joint enterprise. Miles was there when the victim was killed. He was given a twenty-six-year sentence before parole. What would be the rehabilitation? Choose who you associate with? Where he is now, are they the right associates? Zack, also on trial for murder under joint enterprise, told me that he felt sorry for another man who was on trial with him as he was nowhere near the scene of the crime and had no idea that it was going to happen. Again, what would be the rehabilitation? Associates? Hearing these cases on joint enterprise made me look at myself and my life and where I grew up and my 'associates'. I could not help where I was born or brought up or where I went to school. Where I grew up we did not have much money, crime was fun and often passed the time. I was supposed to be aware I had a choice of what direction I took. In the years through my teens that direction was so often lost and the choice of direction for me, most of the time, felt so far away. Years later, upon completing my training and entering my counselling career and the criminal justice system, I felt lucky, and I felt relief. Working with these men, I was aware of where I had come from and the potential of where I could have been. I also felt sadness.

I often heard professionals talk about choices for so many in deprived areas. This is not their reality; choices are few and far between. Often these men lived in houses with no heating or electricity. They would watch their caregiver work every hour but still went hungry. Many men lived in houses where their caregiver was always absent, or if they were present the men only knew severe abuse at their hands. Having gone through all of that they were still expected to be aware they had a choice. Many of the men I worked with said their criminal journeys stemmed from extreme poverty. This, to me, is where it needs to change! Looking around the prison and what counselling offered the men, we were one of the very few services that may have been able to make a difference, the very few services where the people working within it believed they could make a difference to the men's lives and wanted to. The passion and love we have for counselling, I truly feel, was what made it work and build. The men saw the passion we felt for change and rehabilitation, and I feel this enhanced their belief in the service we offered. If only other services were like ours, would our system then change? Would there be less corruption and institutional abuse? If all services had the love and passion that we had would rehabilitation be known within our system?

We had built the service, so counselling was at the heart of it. We knew what counselling could do for the men and we knew how much it was needed. We were also seeing the benefits of counselling in the men, and although it was a tough journey, they were making it. The service was, however, meant to be evidence-based, and more down the psychoeducation route (this being more about working on the men's thoughts and feelings in the here and now, rather than exploring their history). We implemented this into the group work and used the outcome tools that were expected but, for us, it was never about the outcome measures. It was about the men and what worked. We were recruited as two counsellors and that is what we did. We knew, however, that in time this was going to change and the fear it put in us was immense. The thought that we would not have the passion for what we did was an uncertainty and we questioned daily why the service was not recognised for what it was or why it was not looked at from the eyes of "if it is not broken why fix it?" We truly felt that counselling helped men to rehabilitate. It gave them an opportunity to explore and link their lives.

I worked with a man who, over the previous couple of years, had come back and forth into prison. He was caught in the cycle. Logan came into his sessions very anxious. He had previously had counselling, but he said it had not been great and he did not see the point in it. We started to explore his life, and this included his relationship with his parents. Through his sessions, Logan came to realise that he behaved in exactly the way they said he would. Instead of proving his parents wrong, he was, in fact, proving them right. This pattern had led him to prison numerous times over the past two years.

After spending time exploring his relationships deeper and him gaining awareness of the patterns that formed within them, we were then able to speak and explore different situations and his reactions to them. We reflected on his thought process and his emotions and learned to identify with these. We explored how things may look different if his reactions were to change and how he could manage his emotions within different situations. On the day Logan was due to leave prison he said, "I will never see you again, Miss. Thank you for all you have done." The men on the wing were bantering "he will be back" with laughs and more jokes (it was quite common on the wings to hear the men say they will not be back). Logan shouted back, "I won't, counselling has changed my life." He looked at me and said, "You will never understand how much counselling has helped me." I was there for another two and half years and he had not come back. I hope that is the case to this day, and that counselling played a part in his rehabilitation.

Rebecca and I carried on counselling the men with the

same passion we had walked in with, but the imminent change was always within us. We had found our feet within the prison, and we were both happy, but sometimes watching the men find theirs made us feel sad.

Chapter 9
The Sadness of Finding Their Feet

For a man entering the prison for the first time, it is a scary place. The unknowing and the potential danger is immense. Thoughts of whether they would be OK and survive in a place that is known for violence is running through many of the men's heads. Men who have never been in prison before do not know the politics or the dynamics within it. They are unaware of the regime; they do not know where anything is. They are unaware that, in a place like prison, to get something you need or want you need to make a fuss.

They have no clue about the canteen, spends limit and phone pins. They have no idea that the time it takes to receive anything in a prison is more than double that in the community. They do not know that to speak to a GP, mental health practitioner or a dentist, they need to put in an application (otherwise known as an 'app') and the waiting time for this is lengthy. They are unaware that medications taken in the community can be different to those provided in prison and they are not instantly prescribed.

They do not know about induction and that they need to attend this, where they will sit tests in English and Maths and unless they score high, they will not be given a job, they will instead be put in education to get the expected grade. They do not know that if they chose not to attend education, they will spend twenty-three hours behind their door (in their cell). They are unaware of negative IEPS and being put onto a basic regime which includes no association and having their TV removed.

They are unaware that they will go to the induction wing, which is chaotic, loud and dangerous and they will stay there until induction is complete. They will then be moved onto general population. They do not know the different groups and the culture of gang affiliation, they do not know they are entering a wing that has the potential to manipulate their weaknesses and extort them of belongings, canteen and anything else they want.

We would visit the induction wing and be met with many men in need of our help. We knew when a man had not been in prison before; the anxiety would hit us. They would ask so many questions in a short space of time. Men would say, "I really need help, Miss." The disbelief of so many, that they were in prison, was evident as was the feel of a 'deer in headlights'.

Whenever I would work with a man not long after their arrival, the sessions were emotional, themes of wanting to go home and missing their loved ones were overwhelming. The uncertainty of their worlds would open wide in the session. Some men would cry, others would sit, looking bewildered. Many men looked defeated, and they were only at the beginning of their journeys. I would wonder whether counselling helped or whether they needed time to settle into their environment.

When they did settle there were mixed feelings. I remember going to visit a man I had previously seen on the induction wing who was struggling and very nervy, the anxiety taking over him. When I saw Jerome, it was like seeing a different man. He had got to know the system and the environment and was thriving in it. Jerome said to me, "If men only did the first two weeks of their sentence they would never come back." I felt sad to hear this. I felt sad that the men finding their feet meant they were comfortable in a place where no one should want to live or even get used to. I was also saddened as, at times, this was the beginning of a cycle that the man could be in for many years.

It was always sad when Rebecca and I would see a man return to prison after release because we were aware that the cycle for that man had begun and it could take a long time for them to break it. Many men would come back in due to breaching a restraining order. If the man was new to receiving one they would go through the cycle many men had before. They would get a text inviting them round, things would be going great, then they would have an argument and the police were called for breaching the order. Back to prison they came. It was a cycle we had seen and heard numerous times and would use examples of these in our group work. In counselling, we would explore these cycles and the patterns they would follow and discuss what the men might do differently in the hope that we would not see them return.

Drugs was another cycle that was hard to break. Many men were on short sentences, starting with two weeks. Rebecca and I would have conversations about what could be achieved in that time. They would not be clean of drugs within two weeks or even get the opportunity to do any work in prison to try to change this. They would be released into the community pretty much the same way that they entered prison, and the cycle begins again. Whenever we would go and visit the men they would say to us, "It's OK, I know how it works." 'Not my first rodeo' springs to mind. Always saddened me and still does.

Many men joked with us that they had learnt how not to do it, meaning how to not get caught and to be cleverer. This again made me sad, that they had found their feet but in ways to get better at committing crime rather than rehabilitating themselves. Although their comments were meant to be in jest, I knew this was not the case and they had learnt new tricks to their trade. The want from me and Rebecca for the men to never return sometimes felt that we wanted it more than they did, which is a sad thought to have. Men who were frequent returners would make this a joke when they saw us with comments like, "Fancy seeing you here," or "I'm back!" Rebecca and I would hide our disappointment well.

Some men would commit crime purposefully to get put into prison, these were the homeless, during the winter months. I would feel incredibly sad that the only way they felt they could keep warm and get three square meals a day was in a prison. Listening to these men we could understand why, and it was heartbreaking at times. Tough to hear, but it was the harsh reality of someone who is homeless to survive a winter. They knew the system and they knew what they had to do to get into it and which crimes would see them through the winter. They had been to prison many times before and it did not take long to find their feet. One man sat in group and told us how every year while he is homeless this is what he does. He described the harshness of being homeless in the winter and the violence that is on the streets. He said that being in prison provides him with the shelter that he needs. The men in the group looked at me and Rebecca and their anger shone through. They looked at this man, who purposefully put himself in prison just to keep warm, with sadness and disbelief. One man turned to me and said, "Miss, how is that right?" I was unable to answer, as it was not right.

While many prisoners found their feet, Rebecca and I had also found ours. We loved breaking down the stigma and giving the men the opportunity to talk and be heard, but I soon found myself expecting this.

Chapter 10
The Awareness of Expectation

For fifty minutes the men would speak about things they had never spoken about before. They would explore their lives and emotions, work through their traumas, dissect their lost childhoods, and understand their chaotic relationships. The powerful moments in those rooms and the attachments that formed through a trusting, safe relationship with boundaries, were a first for almost all the men I counselled. Many of the men came in and straight away started talking; one young man made me aware it had become my expectation!

I had completed two sessions with Greg and at the end of the second session, I asked him if he felt that he needed counselling. Greg seemed to be aware of himself and was coping well. He did not present with any particular issue and was able to articulate himself and handle himself in confrontational situations. I asked him to have a think about it for our next session. In our third session, Greg said he had thought about it. I was then hit with a question that I did not see coming, a question that would remain with me up until the day I left the prison. Greg asked, "Do you just expect people to come in here without knowing you and just talk?" I remember sitting back in my chair, my hand went to my chin. I was looking at him and it took me a split second to answer, "Yes."

The realisation hit me with force! I had become so used

to the men coming into the room and opening up that I forgot the basic skill of building a relationship. I had become complacent in a place where you are told not to be. After the session, I found myself in disbelief that I felt this way, that my expectation was for everyone to talk. I had not even thought about it. I remember walking into the office and sitting down, turning to Rebecca, and explaining what had happened. I remember continuing this conversation on the way to the gate and the walk to our cars, and I remember thinking about it all the way home.

That one question stayed with me, and it came into every counselling session I had after that. I held it as a unique awareness of expectation. The question had stripped me back to years previous when I was completing my training, when it was all about the basic skills and building a relationship.

Do not get me wrong, men still came into the room and let everything out in one session as though they were not going to get another chance. There were many times that myself or Rebecca would be like, whoa that was a lot today, or that session was intense and overloaded with so much information. We totally understood that these men had all the time in the world to think, and we offered them a space to get those thoughts out and contain and focus them. All the time I held my awareness that some may not and that was OK. I would not say this was easy and at times I did find it difficult. Some men would not say a lot or gave one-word answers. I would ask them their expectation of counselling which they were unable to answer. I would reflect my feeling of being stuck and ask them how they were feeling, and it would be the same. This made me reflect on my expectation of counselling and what it meant for me and the person I was working with. I felt counselling was, in some way, shape or form, intended to help move someone forward if they were given the opportunity to do so, but again this made me question my expectations, especially within the environment I was in.

Rebecca and I often found ourselves thankful that we had studied integrative courses.

If a man is on remand, then he has no way of knowing, most of the time, when his court date is. Uncertainty in the man's life is high and even if he is aware of a date it can be pushed back multiple times. The men only have what their solicitors advise in terms of sentencing guidelines so it is no surprise that they feel stuck. The men on remand are unable to focus on anything other than getting their sentencing out of the way so they know how long they will serve, their release date and transfer possibilities, etc. I learnt to work on the feelings many men had around court, and what their plans were if they were released and we spoke about counselling in the community. We reflected on the sentencing guidelines their solicitors had given and what their goals would be for their journey in prison. We spoke about coping with the sentence, their support networks and opportunities that they could have in prison. We spoke about anxiety and the reasons they felt that way, and how the uncertainty and their environment were major factors. Not seeing their loved ones and often not telling their children where they were took its toll, as did the building they found themselves occupying.

I was aware my expectation of counselling and helping someone move forward in their life was easier for others but not for a man on remand. Day by day men on remand have the same routine, counting down the hours just awaiting their outcome. Many might wait months on remand and during the COVID pandemic, it could be a year. For many men, they felt their lives had been put on hold, the thought of their futures completely unknown, so it is no surprise that the suicide rate for those on remand is much higher than for those who have been sentenced. Counselling the men on remand was hard. Their situations could not be changed; they could not move forward without an outcome of what their futures may look like. What we could do, and did do, was provide them with a space to lay out all their anxieties if they chose to. Again, these men on remand made me reflect on my expectation.

I once worked with a man on remand and it was Martin's first time in prison. He was scared. The fear so evident in his eyes every time he looked up from his hands that were held tightly together in his lap. I will never forget the feelings of helplessness as each week Martin would break down because he had never gone a day without seeing his children. I remember thinking, I cannot change this. All I could do was sit with this man each week as he processed what he was going through. Some months later Martin came up to me on the wing. He seemed in better spirits; he was going to court the following day. He wanted to thank me for what I did for him when he first came into prison in case he went home. I shook his hand and said, "You are welcome." I was unsure of what I had done. Then I remembered I could not change his situation, but I could listen to him. As it turned out, he did go home.

The day I left the prison Greg made me question my expectation of every man entering the room and laying out his life. I said, "You seem angry." He told me he was and then said, "No, actually, I am sad, the good ones always leave, but thank you for all your help." I shook his hand and thanked him and turned away and left the wing. Greg will never know the impact that his question had on me and how he taught me a lesson in the awareness of my expectations: "Do you just expect people to come in here without knowing you and just talk?"

Greg made me remember the conversation Rebecca and I had on one of our many twenty-minute walks back to our cars after the day had ended. That conversation was about the need to conform and the impact it has on the men and how we felt as counsellors.

Katie Carlyon

Chapter 11
The Presumption to Conform

Conforming behaviour seems to be the general idea throughout the system. I never understood why the professionals feel that every man walking into prison should behave and conform to all rules.

The majority do conform but some do not, and I totally understand why. The men I worked with came from backgrounds of neglect, abuse and abandonment. They had learnt behaviours during their lives to survive. Most men had never had rules or boundaries and their relationships with caregivers were chaotic. They were still expected to be told to "Get the fuck behind your door!" and do this with a smile on their face and reply, "Yes, Sir."

While some professionals speak to the men with respect, I have seen the complete opposite. I have seen a lack of understanding and respect and total rudeness and if a man who has lived a life fighting for survival reacts to this it's utter bewilderment. I believe you do not go to work to get hurt but if working in a male prison with violent offenders, surely the expectation of speaking to men with disrespect would be a whack? Of course, there is an element of 'us and them' and it works both ways. To me, the behaviour of the professionals has an impact on the men's behaviour, leading to dislike and high levels of violence on both staff and prisoners alike. You can feel the anger and tension on some wings. Instead of speaking and trying to understand the men, the professionals put them behind their doors for long periods of time for their anger to fester. Many lifers and IPPs would accept this behaviour and walk away, spending hours behind their doors in the hope one day they will be released. They will take the comments, put-downs and disrespect for one reason... their freedom.

Some men are a high risk to staff and these fall within a different bracket. They are generally not interested in working with anyone but overall, many violent men who I had worked with learnt a lot and tried to change their behaviour. The men did not understand themselves. They did not understand where their distorted thoughts had come from and how these had become core beliefs or how their behaviour had been learnt. The men did not understand that their thoughts affect the way they feel which then determines their behaviour and they did not understand that their traumas had infested all areas of their lives. Many of the men felt their lives were normal and their belief to fight if they feel 'mugged off' or threatened was ingrained in them.

I worked with one very violent man. Josh was convicted and originally sent to prison for a violent crime. When he came into prison, he was given another long sentence for a violent assault on another prisoner. Josh entered counselling very mistrusting of me and why I wanted to help him. Over time we built the trust and completed a timeline of his life. He felt there was something wrong with him as violence came naturally to him and he got angry and reacted so quickly. We identified that at the age of three his first memory was violent, and his timeline continued to be an array of violent incidents. This was not an excuse for his violence, it was an understanding of why he reacted so quickly to his anger and his being able to recognise this and understand his life which gave him the opportunity to start working on himself. Which he did. Josh's timeline also showed the different systems he had grown up in, the care system, young offenders' institutions and eventually prison all showing violent assaults, abuse and neglect. He was able to explore his relationships within the systems and with the professionals, gaining more understanding of his trust issues and the eagerness to fight anyone within them.

Relationships, in all forms, did not come easy for many of the men. Trust was huge. We can argue that this could be the same for anyone but in an environment with over six hundred men, and working with at least one hundred at a time, patterns and similarities emerged. Many men grew up with the view to trust no one and especially those in a uniform. Many had not had great experiences with people in authority and these experiences were embedded in their lives. If we think about our basic needs for shelter, food and water, these were not met for many of the men. In certain parts of the prison, shelter was dismal, and I was recommended by numerous members of staff not to drink water from the taps. Food was a major trigger for the men. When things were missing from their canteen or food was missing from their daily meals or meals were completely missed it did not go down too well. While we in the community could go and get food ourselves, the men had to rely on staff to rectify this and very often it was not or they would wait hours for their meal or even staff members would go off shift and not pass the information on. This fuelled anger and mistrust in the men. They would quite often be told the issue would be sorted and later find it had not been. The men, however, were expected not to react to this. They were expected to sit in their cell and wait for however long it took or even just take the feedback on the chin that it had not been done, with a thank you.

The prison system demands the men conform to its rules

and behave accordingly, regardless of whether the idea of conforming defies the instinct and ingrained beliefs of many of the men. There were limited staff interested in listening and negative entries were put to their name on the system, having effects on re-categorising to move on to better prisons and impacting releases. The mistrust that the men had in many circumstances was just being validated even more with every need not being met in the prison.

Many professionals will not think about the men's lives or the reasons behind their instincts to fight. The argument that prison needs to be a punishment for their crimes and the need for the men to conform sadly outweighs the need to understand the men. Many professionals do not understand that the men have built up a mistrust of people who continually let them down over a long period of time and in many cases all their lives.

This was something Rebecca and I worked on within our service. We felt everyone in the prison deserved and needed the opportunity to work on themselves, explore their lives, understand themselves more and understand that many of their behaviours are learnt and they are in a cycle which can be broken. Even though referrals were coming in across the prison, we still sent every man who entered a pack with a self-referral form to have this opportunity.

Chapter 12
Breaking Down Barriers?

Thinking about Equality, Diversity and Inclusion. This was hard within the prison environment. How I worked, I wanted to empower the men to feel more included, accepted, and accepting of themselves and to explore their behaviours to challenge these feelings. In the structure that is a prison system, I questioned how easily this could be done. I worked with men for a short snippet of time out of their overall sentence. I had many questions concerning EDI. How can they be achieved when there is so much discrimination? How can they be achieved when there is oppression? How can they be achieved with so much institutional racism? Ethnic minorities often reported being treated differently and spoken to differently and in many cases this was true. One young man, Harry, walked into our session and described to me how a member of staff asked what he was in for. He did not tell them. The member of staff continued, "I bet you're in a gang. I bet you're from London." The young man of mixed heritage instantly felt the stereotype of what he looks like to others. He felt a mixture of emotions ranging from sadness to anger. Harry said, "I did not quite believe it, but I should." This stirred my emotions and triggered me. I felt angered. I can tell you this man was neither. Harry was from a little sleepy village where the only time you saw a gang was on the TV.

We worked tirelessly to break down the barriers and the

stigma that many men from different cultures and backgrounds felt about counselling. We would walk the wings every day, so the men began to know our faces. We would join in with general chat about how the day was going.

There were certain wings where communities had grouped together. We understood why, but at times this was severe and ended with severe consequences in terms of group-on-group violence. We would promote group to all the men so they had the opportunity to work with others from different backgrounds to foster inclusion, (of course checking the non-associate lists so it was safe to do so). Non-associates were inmates who had been in fights with one another, they may be known to rival gangs, or there could be intelligence on them regarding crime, drug dealing, bullying, etc. Depending on the crime, there was division, for example with drug dealers and drug users. I found it strange how some drug dealers would talk about the users who, in reality, were their customers, calling them names and looking down upon them because of the drugs they took. Men on burglary charges were looked down on while someone who had assaulted his girlfriend was OK. Other times it was vice versa; the dynamic was often confusing as to what crimes were deemed OK and not OK. We would walk towards the vulnerable person wing and often other prisoners would call out to us to not go in there. They would tell us those men did not deserve our help. This wing was for sex offenders, and they were not accepted onto general population. As a rule, across the prison, these are the crimes that are never accepted by many of the men. Group brought together men from across the prison from all different walks of life together (this did not include sex offenders who were offered group separately). For three hours a week for four weeks, they gained an insight into each other's worlds. On many occasions, we were told they would never have spoken to each other if it were not for group. For Rebecca and me, this was the aim. Many men across the prison had one thing in common and that was their mental health.

Gang affiliation divided the prison and many wings. The non-associates spread across the establishment according to where they were from in the community. I remember Rebecca and me facilitating one group session where we were challenging a young man, Dylan, on his 'revenge'. These revenge attacks had been going back and forth for some time and had escalated to very violent acts, including shootings and arson. We listed them on a whiteboard along with his thoughts and feelings at the time. I asked Dylan what would have happened if he had not retaliated the last time. Another member of the group, also a member of a gang but with no links, said, "They don't understand bro, they are from another world." He was right. We could not possibly understand what it was like to be shot at or stabbed. But we wanted to know what it was like for them. We wanted them to not feel judged because they were part of a gang; being judged is something they experience on a day-to-day basis, the acts that they carry out are judged, how they dress is judged, how they speak is judged. We were not there to add to that. We were aware that choice did not come into gang affiliation on many occasions. It is not black and white; it is a complex world to live in. We wanted to give every man in group the opportunity to feel included no matter their history. Dylan replied, "Nah, I want to hear what they have to say."

Many men of colour would report to me the differences in their treatment from that of white men. They said staff were quicker to put men of colour behind their door than they were white men. They would give me examples of when a white man had got into a fight and was still allowed out of his cell. For a man of colour, the consequences for the same behaviour would mean being put on basic (no TV and not being let out for association). I was sitting in a session and Jamie pointed through the door window to another man who was white and said, "See him, he knocked someone out yesterday." I looked through the window and saw the young man jumping around the wing and in that moment, I could not argue with him that he did not have a valid point, and I certainly did not dismiss how he felt. We explored his emotions and how they rubberband him back to childhood years when he grew up with racist slurs and comments aimed at him and his family. I honestly felt sad. I felt sad that the place Jamie now resided in was making him feel the same way he did throughout his childhood. I have heard it within the system of men 'playing the race card' and it annoys me. Why don't you have a conversation with these men to hear for yourself how they are feeling?

The divide that this caused was evident in some of the outbreaks of violence within the prison. It fuelled anger and even though it was the system (and those within it) that caused the divide, they were only ever going to blame each other. We watched as, across the prison, non-associates rocketed and landings were segregated into different groups. Even though we worked with all men within the prison, and no one was excluded from the list, I often questioned myself on where I fell within the system. I questioned whether I was enabling the problem or if I was a part of the problem because I worked within it. I concluded we were there for the men because that was what our belief was. We believed in change, and we believed everyone should be treated equally and fairly and be accepted for who they are. We also both held the belief that counselling should be offered in every segment of our society. No matter where you are or who you are. We were a small part of a very big system, and we would never be able to stop the experiences many of the men went through in terms of oppression, racism and discrimination. As white females, we were aware there are many incidents that we will never be able to understand. But in the men's short snippet of time with our service, they had the space and opportunity for their lives and experiences to be heard, where they could feel accepted and not judged.

We offered counselling to every man that we could. The beauty of counselling and the achievements it can bring to many meant so much to us. We were trained as Integrative Counsellors, meaning we did not offer one specific type of therapy but integrated aspects from different theories, enabling us to work with a broad range of issues. Many of the men we worked with made us question what type of therapy they had previously received.

Chapter 13
Carl Rogers in Prison

When I think of Carl Rogers, the founder of Person-Centred counselling, I think of the core conditions, exploring your patterns of relating and taking steps forward in your life to rid yourself of conditions placed upon you as you were growing up and becoming true to who you are. Anyone in prison, as we know, has their liberty taken away. This is their punishment for their crimes and for breaking the laws of our society, but it does not stop there. They are told when to eat and what to eat. When to shower, exercise, work and educate themselves. How loud to have their music, their voices and their TVs. What to wear on their feet and what to dress in. This raised the question for me, how are these men meant to be true to who they are if they need to conform within a system? My question did not stop there and over time counselling the men raised another question for me. How are they meant to be true to who they are if therapy is teaching them differently?

I counselled men who had come from prisons that were built for therapy. I remember in one session a man spoke about his daughter who was losing direction. Lewis said, "It would never happen if I was out there." He then spent the next ten minutes trying to explain to me what he meant by that. I asked him why he felt he had to spend all that time explaining to me the nature of his words. Lewis described how groups and therapy had been for him. He said if he had used a certain word that seemed 'controlling' or 'aggressive', or if he thought about reacting in a certain situation, he would need to think about it. He explained that everything he said or did, he needed to reflect on. In turn, Lewis's therapy had caused him to be careful with what he said in case it was misconstrued, to be careful how he behaved in case it came across the wrong way. This to me did not feel authentic and made me question therapy in prisons and what was offered to a lot of the men I counselled.

Many of the men I worked with had huge conditions put on them, violence being one of the major factors. Challenging their thoughts and behaviour often turned into an exploration of their childhoods and where this came from. We would complete timelines of their lives showing horrendous traumas. We spent hours dissecting their lives, picking apart pieces of themselves to understand better and create an awareness of themselves. This was not a green light to say their behaviour or actions are acceptable, just an understanding of where it comes from so when they were in situations and are about to react, they are aware. I would hear time and again that men had years of therapy but not like the sessions they had within our service. This really baffled me. Some of these men had spent 20 years in prison! What therapy had they been offered?

The therapy many of the men received had taught them to be clever. It taught them to be able to say the right things, to act in a certain way and it enabled them to jump through the hoops to their release. Being told to go back and think about how they could react or think differently gave them the opportunity to learn what to say in certain situations. Some had years of therapy and they were able to learn this down to a fine art. To me, this is not breaking down the stigma of men and mental health. It did not give the men the beauty that

Carl Roger's theory has to offer. It did not give them autonomy or a chance to be true to who they are, and it did not give them an opportunity to understand themselves or their lives. Instead, it taught them to be what others expected them to be which is what many of the men have been doing all their lives.

I worked with a sex offender, Terry, who was moving on to another prison to complete a course that he needed to before release. We had worked on his crime and his feelings around it and for the victim and their family. We reflected on his life and childhood and his relationships. Many sex offenders had completed the course and had reoffended and come back in. I began to build my own picture of what it was like and always questioned why these men were reoffending. Terry said to me, "I will never reoffend again, I do not have thoughts and do not have no intentions to repeat my crime." In the back of my mind, I was aware that this man would be challenged, he would be deemed unfit and at a high risk of reoffending (whether he would reoffend or not). He would be seen to be in denial which then made me question the course that was offered. If this man truly felt that he would not reoffend, he would still be challenged (rightly so) but would this then cause him to say what he felt he needed to say to complete the course, rather than work on how he actually felt? Which raises another question, how many men have used this course to manipulate the system and be released?

Within my counselling world, this is not congruent and not at all authentic. It is not working from the man's agenda, it is working from the systems, it is not working with what he feels the truth is, it is in fact the opposite. It is giving men the ability to build on manipulation and become cleverer which to me is dangerous.

I worked with a man who presented as 'cocky'. Charlie

87

got along with all the men and staff, he was loud and funny and oozed confidence. He came into counselling with the same air about him as he did on the wing. For the first few sessions, he would narrate his story, skimming over anything traumatic or making a joke of whatever he said. At the end of one of our sessions, I reflected this back to him. Charlie laughed and walked out. In the following session, he acknowledged what I had said to him and added, "You do not tell me what to do." I acknowledged this, I explained to him I was there to listen and not advise, that the sessions were for him to utilise in whichever way he wanted to. Charlie said that he had so many counsellors previously who would advise him, they would not really listen, so he was not used to being heard.

In the sessions to follow I sat back and just listened. The sessions were emotional and at times a lot for him to manage. His life had been a series of traumas filled with abuse and extreme neglect, his relationships were chaotic and toxic, and his parents absent, all of which ultimately led to him trying to take his own life not long before coming into prison. Coming to the end of our counselling I was aware he would be moving prisons, but potentially would be on a short sentence. I asked him how he felt about finding himself a good counsellor in the community. Charlie's response, "I have a good counsellor. I have finally been listened to."

Counselling worked in the prison. It gave the men the chance to be heard. It transformed some of their lives; exploring their histories in a space that is open, honest and non-judgemental was huge for them. Many had never experienced this before.

I often wondered when a man would say "I have never told anyone that before" if this was due to the therapy, as we were working from the man's agenda and his perspectives, not our own. We did not work to monitor outcomes or measure their risk of reoffending. Is this what made many of the men feel they were able to explore their worlds? Whatever it was, we were immensely proud and humbled working with the men and giving them the possibility to eventually move forward to their true selves, aware that their process would be more of a journey than someone in the community and aware that their journey truly began when they were released.

Counselling in a prison is an experience and certainly an experience that stays with you. At times it can be totally different to how you were initially trained, but no matter how much time passes there is one thing that remains the same for a counsellor – their boundaries.

Katie Carlyon

Chapter 14
Firm Boundaries

Working in a prison your boundaries need to be tight. The men can instantly sniff out weakness and will play on this, which is no surprise really as it is their fun time in a place that lacks it. I remember not long after Rebecca started, we walked onto one of the wings and were instantly met with a large group of men standing in conversation. We walked on and said hello. One of the men pointed at me and said, "knows the system" and pointed at Rebecca and said, "doesn't know the system." What the young man did not know was Rebecca's art at firm boundaries. She was misunderstood by many men in her early time but that quickly changed when they began working with her. I had previously worked with offenders, so I had a fair advantage. My demeanour comes from my roots – not an easy neighbourhood – and I feel the men picked up on this and felt a sense of safety and understanding in my presence.

Within counselling our boundaries were tight, as they should be. If the men did not attend a session, they would get a letter advising if they did not attend their next session they would be discharged. One of the men Rebecca was working with came up to me on the wing one day and showed me the letter he had received. I explained in the first session you are advised if you do not attend this would happen. He responded with a big smile on his face, "Yes but I didn't believe she would." It turned out he was used to getting his own way in prison and would easily manipulate situations; he learnt in counselling this was not the case. This was also not the case if the men moved wings. We would tell the men we were working with that, if they chose to move wings because they felt like it, they would be put on the waiting list for counselling on that wing and they would have to wait. Many men tested this, and all the men were shocked that we followed it through. We had gained a reputation for firm boundaries.

I had been working with Brent for six weeks and in one of our sessions he said, "Miss, you do not bend." I asked what he meant by that and he said that I stick to what I have said and went on to explain that many other staff members do not. I explained to Brent that I set out my boundaries in our first session together and again his response was, "I did not think you would stick to them."

Sometimes boundaries do slip and with one man I realised this was happening. For some reason they were not firm from the moment that Billy stepped out of the laundry room, his loud laugh and voice penetrating the whole wing. He would still be asleep every morning that I went along for our session, but I would wait for him. I would also tell him off for his bad behaviour. I would follow him from wing to wing. I had gone into parent state with this man. I was aware that I was speaking to him like I would my child. There was something about him that I found needed to be looked after and guided. Billy had been in prison a very long time and was battling against the system, I knew that he would carry on losing and potentially never go home. I visited him one day and I asked him if he felt I spoke to him like a child. He laughed the laugh that every man and staff member knew, and he said, "Yes, because I act like a child." From that moment on I held my awareness of my parenting feelings towards this man. He later re-referred into counselling. I did not work with him, knowing the motherly feelings I felt towards him. I kept my boundaries firm.

I was once speaking to a group of men on the wing and one of them said, "You are straight down the line aren't you Miss? You're not bent." I turned around and said, "No, I am not bent/ Would you want to speak to me as your counsellor if I was bent?" I noticed the group of men all thinking about it, nodding their heads with mumbles of "true".

While I was walking across the wing one day a man stepped out of his cell on the landing above with just a pair of shorts on. Ali was well known for pushing boundaries. He shouted down, "Miss, where am I on the waiting list?" I did not stop walking, looked up at him and shouted back, "Put some clothes on and I will speak to you." Behind me I heard laughs from the other men who were looking on and most probably waiting to see if I would interact with a half-naked man. As I said, we held firm boundaries.

One of the men on Rebecca's wing tried to test her boundaries on the landing. She was speaking with a group and as she walked off one of them said, "I love you." Rebecca turned back and walked up to him and pulled him to the side and said, "Are you aware of how that makes me feel when you say inappropriate things like that?" The man went red, he could not get his words out. These men usually got ignored for shouting things out. They were not used to being asked about their behaviour. What he did say to Rebecca was how sorry he was, and it was not his intention to make her feel a certain way. As it turns out he never told her he loved her again.

On one of our walks home to the gate, Rebecca and I were reflecting on our day when one of the men I was working with shouted out the window, "I miss you!" I made a mental note and in our next session I asked him if he missed me. Colin did not know what to say or how to respond. I asked him whether the reason he missed me was why he felt he had to shout it out as I walked past. Colin started to laugh but it was a nervous one, then he sat back and said, "I'm sorry, Miss, it won't happen again." And it didn't.

In the summer for Rebecca and me it was a transition. We would walk the grounds in big coats and huge thick cardigans for however long we could. We would eventually need to change into summer clothes. I always felt bare just in trousers and a t-shirt and this did not go unmissed by the men. I walked onto the wing one day and I was walking across the landing when a man said, "Miss! Dam, you look different, thank God for summer, aye boys!" and started to laugh. I did not find this funny. I walked over to him and told him his comment has made me feel uncomfortable. He genuinely looked horrified, and repeated "Sorry, Miss" numerous times. I accepted this and turned and walked away, knowing he would in future keep his opinions to himself.

Even though these things were relatively small and not derogatory, they were still not acceptable. Rebecca and I, if safe to do so, would have a conversation with the men to let them know that inappropriate comments or behaviour were not going to be ignored by us. I feel that this contributed to the service and the reputation that we had. In the whole time I worked there, we did not receive one complaint and that is because we stuck by the golden rule: if you say you're going to do something, do it. In the grand scheme of things and working in the prison, between myself and Rebecca, we had experienced worse comments walking along the street than what we did in there. As time went on, our reputation grew and the comments became fewer and fewer.

Boundaries sometimes needed to be even firmer,

especially when you have multiple personalities sitting in front of you. Once a week that was what we had, in what we called 'our group'.

Katie Carlyon

Chapter 15
The Power of Group Work

Once a week Rebecca and I would make our way from our office armed with a bag of group materials, a kettle, plastic cups, tea, coffee and biscuits. From the very first group with Dave, running groups was always nerve-wracking. You never knew who or how many would walk through the door. Having set up the group with a room booked out each week, the sessions needed to fit in with the prison regime and mass moves. Mass move is when all the men are moved at once. In the morning they move to their place of work, education, group, induction, etc. Three and a half hours later, they would all move back.

Due to the men not being able to move back whenever they wanted to, we tailored the groups. Instead of twelve one-hour sessions each week, they were doing four three-hour sessions. So for the next four weeks, we would have the same men in group. Our concern was that the men would get bored; three hours was a long time for them to sit in group. However, we were aware there was no alternative and if they did attend for an hour they would still have to wait the rest of the time until mass move began again. There were men who could not sit there for three hours and that was OK. We made it clear at the beginning of the group that it was not mandatory and that they did not have to stay and attend. Some men left at that point but many stayed. Some men left due to the idea of group being too much for them, but we always reassured them that they were still on the counselling waiting list. We ensured we put breaks within the three hours where we would make them tea or coffee and hand out some biscuits.

Group worked and our attendance rates soared as did the number of men attending. All men were on our waiting list for counselling so by the end of the four weeks they did not have much time to wait before their sessions commenced. There are many memories of group, including watching connections form between men from across the prison. Many of the men would not have met each other on their journeys but group gave them the opportunity to do just that. The moment that it dropped for the men and a light bulb seemed to go off – when they understood the links and little things started to fall into place, whether it was understanding the sensations within them coming from their anxiety or the way the brain works and acts as a defence mechanism going into flight, fight or freeze – was one of the many reasons we loved our jobs. Watching how thoughts, emotions and behaviours connected a group of men from many different backgrounds, beliefs and cultures was something special. The empathy that was conveyed in the room between them, because they had similar experiences in terms of their mental health, was something amazing to witness. Challenging thoughts and looking at other ways to view a situation, and watching all get involved, I will never forget. I often stepped back and would make eye contact with Rebecca, small smiles on both of our faces.

There were times in the group which were challenging and some of the men thrived on this. An older man once challenged me and Rebecca on how to not self-harm anymore. Connor had self-harmed for many years and had been in so many different therapies to try to overcome it. He made it quite clear that our service would not help him, and I made it clear he did not have to be there. Connor stayed and he attended the next week's course. So did another young man who did not appear to be OK. Shaun seemed very different to the week before. The men were asking Shaun if he was alright as Rebecca and I were getting prepared. Shaun explained that he had tied his bedding together and had the intention of ending his life when he was taken back to his cell.

I ran that group alone while Rebecca spent the morning getting Shaun the help he needed. I checked in individually with the group, as to how they each felt. We spent the session reflecting on suicide and self-harm and the impact it has. Shaun did not end his life and he did not come back to group. He had a tough few months ahead of him while his mental health was stabilised. Rebecca and I would check in with him weekly. At the end of the group, we gave the men feedback forms to complete and, as always, we asked for honesty. We advised the men that for our service to grow and get better we needed the critiqued feedback as well as the good. Connor's feedback remains with us to this day: "I watched this service save a life."

While running group you must be aware of the many different personalities within it. In nearly every group we would have an angry man. In one group, the angry man had looked at his thoughts, emotions and behaviours and how they could be challenged. He basically concluded his behaviour was right. He would give his wife a slap if she made him feel a certain way. I challenged him. As I continued to challenge him, he said, "I feel like smashing this place up." I told him, "Well done for not reacting." By the end of the session, Rebecca and I debated whether to have this man in the group. He took up a lot of the others' time by arguing his point and any other point he could find. We could feel the tension within the group which was something relatively new to us. I knew when the man got angry a few of the other members wanted to react but did not. A few days later I saw the man and he stopped me. He said he felt group was not for him and he would wait for his counselling sessions. I remember feeling a sense of relief!

Rebecca and I were walking through the gate to go home one day and were suddenly faced with the angry gentleman sitting on the bench. I was shocked as we were not aware he had been released as he had not started his counselling. I was unsure how the conversation would go following group. The man stood up from the bench and walked up to me and put out his hand. I offered my hand and he shook it, all the while thanking me for what I did in the group. He said he had needed it and that it made him think a lot, and that he felt he was ready for change and was starting counselling in the community.

Even though many of the men wanted counselling and were always saying they wanted one-to-ones, we saw the benefits of group. It built relationships, inclusion, acceptance and understanding. Group also gave us the opportunity to build up a relationship for when the men entered one-to-one counselling, as many were wary. It gave the men an understanding of themselves and a space to decide whether therapy was for them and whether they were ready to delve into their lives and make small changes to them.

In a sense, group gave the men a safety net with others around them but when it was two people in a room, sometimes they were not willing to drop their defence and that was their unique way of survival.

Chapter 16
The Art of Survival

In the counselling sessions, I would often feel the men were not being totally honest, as though they were holding something back. It felt like they were giving me something, but it did not feel whole. Upon reflection, I understand why I may have felt that way.

Prison is an environment where, if you present as weak, you will be targeted. This could take the form of being attacked, bullied and/or extorted (just to mention a few). I was asking the men to come into the counselling room and be vulnerable, break down their defences, including bravado, which in turn meant I was asking them to break down their safety net, their protection and their survival mechanism.

To me, these men walked around with baggage, that baggage being their lives, heavily loaded with trauma, grief, depression and anxiety. I was asking them to give their baggage to me. While they gave me some of their baggage, the part they held back allowed the men to still have a safety net, a defence and a survival mechanism so they were able to navigate and survive in their environment. The men were keeping themselves safe.

I worked with a young offender who was very loud, always dancing, laughing and bantering. Oliver would come into our sessions laughing and joking. Whatever area of his life that we explored he seemed OK with. His life in care, his prison history and his absent father was all described by him as "it is what it is". This made me ask myself how am I even helping this person? I worked with Oliver for twelve weeks before he was transferred. He spoke about surface-level issues. While exploring his life, something within me was always saying don't go too deep with him, do not challenge him too heavily. He walked out of our sessions every week with the same bravado as he entered. Some while later, and on reflection, I realised I had helped him. I had helped this person by not breaking down his bravado – what I had seen and felt was a potentially vulnerable young man whose bravado was his defence.

Unconsciously, I was aware that if he broke that defence down, what did he have in a place that was dangerous, violent and dog-eat-dog? Not pushing him to go deeper into his history kept Oliver safe. This realisation made me feel sad and reverted me back to my feeling of the men not being honest and holding things back. Counselling is based around helping people explore areas of their lives to move forward and become more true to themselves, but how are these men meant to be true to who they are when they are constantly in survival mode?

We worked with many men who had never imagined themselves sitting in front of a counsellor. To me these men seemed more vulnerable, they had never acknowledged their mental health and had quite often grown up in a 'man's man' home where crying was for girls. Being the big strong man was inbred in them; it was their survival. We saw how this had a huge effect on many men when they arrived in prison. Their lives had stopped going around and they had to get off and their mental health was soon felt. There is not much to do in prison and even if you are lucky enough to have a job, it is still only six hours of your day and the rest is spent in your cell. I remember two men in particular who I worked with, both 'strong men', had never given their mental health a look-in, but unconsciously knew something was there. Another thing they both had in common was the question I would ask them at the end of every session, "Have you had thoughts of suicide?"

Tim, at the beginning of his counselling journey, asked me if he had to answer that question. I replied that I would not force him to do so but still needed to ensure he was safe, that he had no intention of ending his life. Just the thought of saying he had thoughts of suicide was breaking down a defence for him and potentially opening up the floodgates. By not answering this question Tim was protecting himself from looking deeper into those thoughts. If those floodgates fully opened, could he survive going through them in prison?

Karl, in one of his sessions, when asked the same question, put his two fingers on the edge of the table in a V sign and said he had always felt his life was like this. He tilted his fingers a little bit over but never let go of the table and said this to me with tears in his eyes. The following week Karl asked if we could skip this question. I advised we could, but I still had to ensure he was safe, that he also had no intention of ending his life.

Anyone looking at these two men would have had no clue what turmoil they were in within themselves. They showed no inclination on the wing or at their places of work. They just carried on carrying their hidden baggage.

I was often asked by staff members, do you think they honestly need counselling? Don't you think it's for other reasons that they want to attend? I would never answer them. It angered me to start off with so the answer I would have given would have been far from professional. To me, this showed how well many men hid their mental health and their feelings within the system and showed me that mental health still was not understood, especially the stigma of men in prison. It angered me that staff did not seem to understand how big it was for many men to walk into our counselling room and give parts of themselves to us. It angered me that they felt the need to question whether I felt the men really needed it, as if we were too naïve to realise that some men would access the service to sit in a room with a female for fifty minutes, and we had worked with some.

Gareth had attended the twelve-hour group we ran. He did well and helped and challenged me in it. He was now at the top of the waiting list for one-to-one counselling. I went to visit him armed with his letter that advised his start date and time. I asked him if he still wanted counselling. Gareth smiled, looking a little coy and said, "Do you know what, Miss? I don't, I am going to be truthful. I was not in it for the right reasons and thought you two may be corrupt but you are not." My words back to him were, "Thank you for your honesty, it is refreshing."

The moment a man walks into a room there is a sense of why they are there. Rebecca and I both worked openly and honestly and many of the men got a shock when they came into counselling and saw how boundaries work. It was almost like you could feel the shift in dynamics within minutes of the session beginning as they realised what it was and definitely what it was not.

I remember Stewart walking into my session and as he sat down, I got that feeling. The dynamic did not shift as quickly as it normally would have so I brought it into the room. I said to Stewart that attraction is normal between male and female and asked him if that was the case with him. If it was, we could work on it. I felt the dynamic I was so used to shift, his reply, "Na Miss." Our work could begin.

I also wondered if this was another means of survival for the men. As two counsellors within the prison, we were well-known. Whoever entered and left our room, which was located on the landings of the wings, other men would know why. What did they say to the other men who knew they were having counselling? Did they make light of it? Or pretend they were having counselling because of the female company? Rebecca and I will never know the answer.

I came to the conclusion that to survive in prison the men could not give all of themselves within counselling. They could give just enough to explore and to gain some clarity, enough to make small changes, enough to take steps forward and enough to build some level of awareness about themselves… but they held back enough of themselves to survive the system and environment that many of them would spend years living in… and that is OK.

Unknown to anyone in the prison, or even the whole world, something was soon going to hit that would put every person into survival mode… COVID-19.

Chapter 17
The Forgotten

COVID-19 was a horrendous time for so many. People were losing their loved ones, nearest and dearest were becoming ill, mental health deteriorated, domestic abuse skyrocketed. There were PPE shortages, food shortages and people losing their businesses. The NHS was finally celebrated for their hard work which previously went unnoticed. All of it was documented and filtered into our homes via news channels and social media platforms. I, however, do not remember one single mention of those who worked or lived in prison.

Walking into the prison I felt a sense of responsibility. The anxiety I had, of potentially carrying COVID-19 into the prison and infecting others, was real! I carried around a pocket-size hand sanitiser and walked the grounds in a mask. Counselling had stopped! My first thoughts were the effect this would have on the men accessing the service. The hard work soon began!

From the first week of lockdown, Rebecca and I put together packs to be sent out to the men on our caseload and those waiting. Within the first week, we had sent out one hundred and fifty packs. Every day we would stand at the photocopier, after our daily struggle to find one that worked. For hours on end, we would photocopy cell packs on anxiety, coping strategies, mindfulness, pictures to colour in, origami, lessons in beginners' yoga (men doing the poses of course), the list went on. We purchased puzzle books to send out and reading books that we felt would help the men. We purchased colouring pencils so they could colour in and stress balls for when times became too much. Eventually, the phone lines were put in so we could phone the men directly. We were unable to offer confidential counselling due to the line being monitored; the line was only for those working within the prison. I remember many of the men saying I had scared them as they had not heard a phone ring in so long and did not think it worked. We then got a list of all the in-cell phones within the prison. Within ten days we had phoned our caseload plus two hundred and fifty men. By the end of the three weeks, we had called the whole prison and had a list of all the men who wanted weekly check-ins. We continued to send our packs to every man who entered the prison. The numbers were so high and to this day I think we stopped counting at around six hundred and fifty. Many on my caseload did not trust the line and would unplug it for fear of it being 'bugged'. If we were permitted to go on the wing, I would go to their door and give a time and day I would call so they could plug it in.

The in-cell calls lasted six months. Within that time the men had gone through an extreme lockdown of around sixteen days, and the anger had festered. The men did not leave their cells, they did not exercise, associate, clean their bedding/clothing or shower. They were given their food through the door. Many of the men I spoke to deteriorated in terms of their mental health. Their lack of understanding of what was happening within the prison was evident. No one advised them or answered any of their questions until much time had passed and then it was too late. We would continue to call and send whatever they needed, and we would speak about coping techniques and mindfulness on a daily basis. Always in the back of our minds was the urge to get back to what we did best… counselling.

During this time, our organisation had won a bid to continue the contract. We were over the moon but it was short-lived as it would not be the service we had built. The contract was mainly around psychoeducation work, looking at thoughts, emotions and behaviours, and it did not include counselling. The service would be going in a direction that I was not happy with. I was aware that now the bid had been won, the change would be set in motion quickly. I knew that in the future I would have a big decision to make about whether I stay. Rebecca did also. For the time being, we would keep that in the background and focus on our jobs.

Six months after COVID-19 hit the country we were allowed to offer counselling on certain wings. I remember the excitement of being able to do our jobs again! I also remember wondering what it would be like counselling the men I had been checking in with weekly, aware that the dynamics would be so different. I remember meeting the men I had only ever spoken to over the phone and introducing myself as 'the person you spoke on the phone to every week' and feeling the gratitude and appreciation from their 'Thank you, Miss'.

Twelve weeks after we began counselling, the prison locked down again. For the next three months, it was time to go back to the in-cell phones and the photocopier. Eventually, a year later, we slowly moved out of the lockdown. Visits were still not permitted face to face and the gym was still closed, education was non-existent and only the kitchen staff went to work. There were no transfers out of the prison. A lot of the men had been in there for a couple of years and were ready to go to another prison. Many men were awaiting a transfer to an open prison but were still under the harsh conditions of twenty-three and a half hours of lockdown. Restrictions were tough and not seeing their family members was hard. They spent most of the time in their cells. Many of the men had experienced deaths outside of the prison that they were unable to mourn. Self-harm had increased as did suicidal ideation. The men were seeing the community being able to mix and everything opening back up and could not understand why the prison was still majorly locked down. High numbers of staff had come down with COVID, some extreme cases. Staff shortages added to the reasons the prison was not able to open up. Many of the men felt the staff liked it that way and felt they had no intentions of prison life going back to the way it was.

To me, the prison felt different as did the men in it. Before COVID, our service was thriving with group work that had gone to twice a week due to high numbers. We would counsel five men per day plus complete up to four assessments. The effects of COVID-19 were evident in the men. It was the hardest sentence that they would ever do. Counselling the men had shifted. COVID had taken a huge toll and the amount of time they were behind their doors had major effects on their mental health. The counselling sessions were used as a space to process the last year and their feelings about their futures. The uncertainty COVID had brought raised anxieties across an establishment that did not need anymore.

All the while Rebecca and I were also getting used to our new world and the changes within it. There were times when I did not feel like the counsellor that I used to be pre-COVID. I knew this was not the men. The driving force of changing our service was changing me. I was a walking contradiction in the prison and Rebecca felt the same. Counsellors were no longer wanted but that was what we were; we were not practitioners who ran psychoeducation sessions.

(psychoeducation sessions being predominately based on thoughts, feelings and behaviours, providing information and homework around mental health). It was taking its toll. I was losing my bounce in a place that was my dream to be in and while I was losing my bounce many of the men were losing theirs.

Most of the men wanted out. They were hearing other prisons had opened up in terms of regime, visits and the gym. We were aware many of the men, mentally, needed things to open up again. The men wanted transfers.

Katie Carlyon

Chapter 18
The Transfer

Some men wanted to transfer, or ship, and others did not. There are numerous factors in transferring, ranging from how far away the men are from their families to the category of the prison. There is also the case of gang affiliation and non-associates for some. Most men wanted to get to a category D prison, which is an open prison, and would focus on navigating themselves through the system to get there. Some men on long-term sentences would work hard to get themselves into therapeutic communities or progressive moves, making it easier for them to get released.

We were always happy for the men if they were transferred to the prison they felt would be good for them. In these cases, it was easy to navigate our counselling as we had a rough estimate of the number of sessions there would be. There were many times when transfers were an issue for us due to the men being halfway through their therapy. There were times I would have one session with a man to then find the next week he was gone. This was something we had to accept. The men were not put on hold until completion of their counselling so there were many times when we would go to the wings and find that they had been transferred out. Our feelings were always around the harm that this could cause.

When I was relatively new into the prison I was working with a young man who had been given a long sentence. It was Blake's first time in prison. His life had been hard. His offence had been violent, triggered by years of racism. He could not believe his own actions and we were exploring this. I went on the wing to get Blake for his session, and I was told he had been transferred. I remember my feelings of panic. This young man had so much trauma and had just begun to explore this and he had been shipped! I was left not knowing what would become of him or even if he was OK. I've often wondered what his journey in prison has been like, to this day I still do not know.

We tried different ways to keep the men in the prison while we worked with them, but due to the high numbers of men coming in they needed to transfer out. We were often left with questions. Are they OK? How are they getting on? Have they managed to access counselling where they are? We had no way of knowing. We questioned the safety of counselling and how we could ensure that the men had an ending to their sessions no matter how many they had. As we got to know the system and the dynamics of how it worked, we got a rough understanding of when the men may be transferred. The men would also let us know if they had put in for a transfer or whether their offender manager had advised they were on the list. This gave us the warning and we would ensure that the sessions we had with the men all had an ending leading up to their transfer. We would discuss different options and help they could receive in other prisons and would speak about counselling in the community. We would explore their feelings around endings and how they felt about endings in general, exactly like we would if they were at the end of their sessions.

We would often go and say goodbye to the men on our caseloads if we were made aware they were being transferred. There were times we made it and times that we did not, and we would walk away feeling a little deflated when we did not make it in time. There was always the same conversation between Rebecca and me, hoping the man would be OK.

Post-COVID was a strange time. Rebecca and I were finally saying goodbye to some of the men we had worked with across a two- to three-year period. Due to COVID, the men stayed in the prison longer and many were able to complete the twelve hour-long group sessions and access their sixteen sessions of counselling. Some men had more due to the gap in the counselling, so started again from the beginning. We had also spoken to the men on a weekly basis for six months while they were in lockdown. The relationships that were built were those of trust and understanding. For us to see the men shipped felt emotional. Many of the men we worked with were serving long sentences and the change we saw from when we first started with them to speaking to them in the holding cell, , was amazing. Many of the men had worked so hard in the time we worked with them, in all aspects of their lives. Their journeys were not easy, and they were thrown curve balls and jumped hurdles to be where they were. We were proud of the men.

The goodbyes for us were good luck! We hoped they continued doing what they were doing and would have the easiest journey possible through the system. We were also not naïve enough to know that many of the men in the background may have been involved in some sort of criminal activity, for example, accessing mobile phones but if they were involved in some form of behaviour, they never let us know. It never affected the work they did within the sessions because they worked on themselves, their fears, anxieties, trauma and bereavements, which at times caused issues for us with staff members as they were more aware of criminal activity than we were, but we were there as counsellors. These men also highlighted what the service was; they were the men who were a part of an upcoming service, a service that had become known across the whole of the prison and these men had had the beauty of counselling pre-COVID as well as the group work offered. They had moved on to pastures new which is where we found ourselves heading also.

We received letters from some of the men who transferred out and they would let us know how they were doing. Rebecca and I would always be so excited to open them and read them. We would smile and laugh at some of the things that they had written relating to their time in prison and working with us. We also felt proud when they said they were keeping their heads down and really trying to keep out of trouble. We would feel humbled when they thanked us for our help and described what that help had meant to them. We were unable to reply (not that we did not want to) and always hoped that they understood why we couldn't, but we felt happy for the men, knowing they were heading in the right direction in their journeys.

Following COVID, our organisation was full steam ahead for the direction they wanted the service to go in. It felt to me that our service was beginning to come to an end and with the familiar faces having left the prison it felt somewhat like an omen. Rebecca and I often had conversations in terms of how we felt and what we were going to do. We loved our service so much, but we were aware that it was not the same as it was before and going forward would not be like it again. There were times you could say that we were in denial, trying to ignore the inevitable that was surrounding us, but everything intensified.

I came to my conclusion, and it was time to reflect on some of the work that I did in a place that will always have a piece of me.

Chapter 19
The Intensity of Therapy

The work I did with the men was the most important thing to me, as it was for Rebecca with her work. I loved every second of it. Counselling the men, the trust seemed to build relatively quickly as did the forming of the therapeutic relationship and the mutual respect and understanding. Therapy was intense with many of the men I worked with. Upon reflection, I sat back and thought about the hours I had spent in those rooms doing the job that I love, and it rose pride in me, especially for the men who had worked so hard.

One of the very first men I worked with had a diagnosis of borderline personality disorder and was stuck in a cycle of breaching restraining orders due to his 'caring' nature. Jack came back into prison time and again, what is known as the revolving door. Working through his therapy he had no idea of his diagnosis or the behaviours that come with that. We explored these, and he identified with many on the list. To see the realisation that it is related to his diagnosis was heartfelt. Jack would drive his car at high speeds down the motorway, not wanting to kill himself but to get the feeling that it gave him. He felt, at times, he was crazy. Jack would want his girlfriend to message him on every step of her night out, so he knew what she was doing and where she was. In his reality, this was to protect her, but in her reality, she felt controlled and unsafe. His relationships were chaotic and his thoughts of self-harm immense. He felt emotions ten times stronger than the average person would, and he would fleet between anger and sadness and not know how to control them. We worked for hours on the areas of his life he felt needed the most work. For me, being able to witness Jack's awareness of himself and how he relates in a relationship build was humbling. He worked hard in his sessions to build on this. When he did leave the prison, he went with a unique awareness of his patterns in relationships and with coping skills to help him manage his emotions and with more of a belief that he would not return as he had before.

I worked with another man who came into his session and said, "I do not know who I am." Marcus had spent so many years in prison, he felt lost and did not know himself. The following session we looked at his comment about not knowing himself and we stripped him back to basics and his favourites in life. I asked him if he had a favourite car. Favourite type of music? Favourite football team? Favourite food? Favourite colour? After each answer he gave me, I asked him the same question, "Has that always been your favourite since you can remember?" His answer each time was yes. Watching Marcus smile and hearing him laugh for the first time throughout that session will always stay with me. For him, the realisation of the simple things gave him a little bit of hope that he had not lost all of who he was in the system. From that session onwards Marcus kept growing, in terms of getting to know himself. When he finally transferred on to another prison, he was aware of what he needed to do and who he was and started to prepare for his journey for release.

I worked with Jayden whose anxiety was immense. His anxiety predominately being around relationships. Jayden did not trust very easily and felt that the person he was in a relationship with would be unfaithful. It was hard for him to think that may not be the case. His anxiety was off the scoring chart, so we began our work. We spent his sessions exploring his previous relationships and how these were often filled with violence and infidelity on both sides. We explored Jayden's family relationships and then explored how he viewed his parents. His mum had an affair with another man, which caused violence within his parents' relationship. It became a cycle; this is what he had learnt growing up about how relationships worked. As the sessions moved on and he had linked his views of his relationships and his patterns that he returned to time and again, we were able to focus on his relationship at the time. He worked hard, he journalled and recorded his thoughts, and he learnt to challenge them when he was alone. As the weeks passed his anxiety reduced and reduced, until one day he came into his session, in total shock and said, "My anxiety has gone." Following our sessions, Jayden carried on challenging himself and was able to keep his anxiety levels low. He was one of the men who would send every man he could into our counselling service.

I worked with Bobby who came into his sessions like he had no care in the world. It was not like that at all. Bobby carried with him a lifetime of traumas, shootings, stabbings and deaths. This had been his world all his life. In his sessions, we worked mainly around identifying his emotions which he had spent most of his life suppressing. We explored different emotions and linked them to various stages and events in his life. Throughout Bobby's sessions, I noticed he smiled constantly, especially when he would speak about traumatic events he had endured. I reflected this back to him. This piece of reflection stayed with this young man. He was released from prison (we were aware he was coming back due to a pending case). When Bobby did arrive back at the prison months later, he approached our service and said what I had reflected in his session about always smiling had stayed with him. It had impacted him so much that he had put himself onto a counselling list in the community. That one session stayed with Bobby for months. He was soon transferred to another prison. I truly hope that one piece stays with him. There is always the possibility he will think about going back into counselling once his prison journey finally ends.

There are many instances of counselling that I could write about where we had an impact on someone's life and mine. The beauty of the career I chose came through repeatedly as I watched the men not only on their counselling journeys but also on their prison journeys. There is no better feeling than knowing that a man you worked with, his direction lost, found his way forward and found a sense of purpose in a place that can swallow you whole. There is no better feeling than hearing that someone whose whole world revolved around finding the next drug to take, was still not taking drugs on the outside and was doing well. There is no better feeling than hearing that a man you worked with is no longer homeless and has been given accommodation in a new area, after years of prison visits, transforming his life. There is no better feeling than finding out years later that a man you had worked with for a long time, whose life was consumed with anxiety and the need to get home to his 'missus' and children but faced years ahead of him, navigating himself through the categories of the system, finally got his category D status, meaning he would get town and home visits, see his family regularly, giving him some sense of normality for the rest of his sentence.

These are some of the reasons why I bounced around the prison with a huge smile on my face, excited for each day ahead, believing in change and finding a purpose deep within a person.

As I said, the organisation had other ideas. Having reflected on some of my work, it was now time to reflect on my moment in time.

Katie Carlyon

Chapter 20
My Moment in Time

My time in the prison will always be the best years of my career. I feel very humbled and grateful to all the men I worked with for allowing me insight into their lives and this will always stay with me. I could not tell you how many men we counselled over the years or how many attended our groups, all I can say is the prison and the men taught me a lot. The men opened up their worlds and gave us a look into their lives which were filled with pain and sorrow. Each man walking those grounds carries something within them and whether they kept it in or sat in our room and explored it, within those walls you can feel it. Prison will always be the saddest place I have known.

The prison and men will hold a special place in my heart most probably until my last days on Earth. It was not just my place of work but my dream. From the time I was studying to qualify as a counsellor, prison was where I wanted to be. You would be quite right to wonder who would say that. But it was my dream to work as a counsellor in a prison, and I did that. I lived my dream. It exceeded my expectations and will be a place I will never forget.

Prison is a toxic environment, an environment within a system that sometimes felt like it was still in the 1900s and a system that I questioned daily. A system I had lost trust in and myself on the other side of the fence. It had become easier for me to say who the good people within the system were and I watched as violence rates soared and could feel the anger and tension across the whole establishment. I watched as self-harm rose and drug use rocketed and there was absolutely nothing anyone could do.

Prison holds so much trauma, sadness, violence, hate, aggression, self-harm, suicide, neglect and abuse, the list is endless and it will not have many positive acts on it. I can say now that working in the prison was a moment in time for me. Granted, that time was some of the best work I did, but it was also a time when I was caught up in what I call a whirlwind. Those years lifted me up and flew me around the prison so quickly my feet did not touch the floor. Daily self-harm, alarm bells and suicide bells became normal as did the violence and aggression. I was becoming desensitised to violent acts without even knowing it. I did not seem affected in my personal life by acts of violence on the TV like my family and friends were, it had become my 'norm'.

With all that, we were still growing and building, a service that had gained such a great reputation. The referrals came in thick and fast, and we were working with so many men offering different interventions: in-cell work, reading lists, distraction packs and of course counselling. When I look back at my time and all that I witnessed, heard, thought and felt, my time was more like triple what I did but in reality it was only three years and four months.

While the service had been established, I was handling the politics of the system and the organisation I worked within and the powers higher than myself. I was fighting to save a service from becoming something I did not believe in, a service that I did not build. As I previously mentioned the organisation was going down a route that no longer included counselling and I was fighting for the men and fighting to keep counselling within the prison. My fight was coming to